Santa Clara County Free Library

REFERENCE

 5816

MUSICIANS TALK

The Theatre

MUSICIANS
TALK

By

Mrs LEONORA (WOOD) ARMSBY

*Managing Director of the Philharmonic Society
of San Mateo County, California*

DIAL PRESS, INC.
NEW YORK   MCMXXXV

PRINTED IN THE UNITED STATES OF AMERICA
BY THE VAIL-BALLOU PRESS, INC., BINGHAMTON, N. Y.

To

*The loyal friends of the Philharmonic Society of
San Mateo County, whose goodwill and per-
severance have enabled us to achieve
our aims and to maintain our ideals.*

PREFACE

FOR ten summers, a series of open-air concerts by a picked orchestra have been given at the Woodland Theatre in San Mateo. These concerts have succeeded while other and more pretentious orchestral seasons have failed. In the successive years they have gathered strength and attracted a constantly larger following. A number of the most prominent orchestral conductors of the world have directed them. The programs have been carefully chosen, partly with a view to enlisting the interests of a wide public, but always with the intention of purveying significant music. Those who have attended the concerts—and their numbers are thousands—have acquired, without fuss or feathers, without being subjected to oppressive methods of instruction, a very profitable and pleasurable acquaintance with orchestral literature.

A task of this kind is only accomplished by means of unfaltering idealism, energy, tact, and clearness of purpose. Orchestral enterprises are constantly attempted in this country. A few succeed. Most of them fail. Very few of them are self-sustaining, and fewer still enlist the active support of the community as a whole. The one in the Woodland Theatre has attained these objectives. As in most cases, the achievement is essentially the conception and the work of an individual. Mrs. Armsby, with a fineness of purpose and a singleness of mind past praise, has worked to such purpose that not only has she experienced the results of her own labors, but has convinced an entire community, from its most influential to its least conspicuous members, of the desirability and need of the orchestral concerts she instituted. She has done this by keeping her promises, and by supplying something beautiful and precious that her public found it wanted. Others about her were quick to coöperate, either from previous knowledge of her character, or because practical results followed so swiftly and surely upon her efforts. Because of them the symphony concerts in the Woodland Theatre have continued through good times and bad, and have had the unfailing support of deeply interested patrons.

In this book she has cited none of the achievements that she might have enumerated. She has followed unconsciously the remark of the news-

paper editor, that "the best stories are those we
don't print." The drama back of the concerts is
concealed from the public gaze. The battles fought
and won by patience, sagacity, unalterable determination and inviolable artistic aims, are here
unmentioned. The scenes in this book are the
pleasant ones that come after the battle—casual
conversations that occurred between performances
or in the hours when the participants were off duty
and off guard, and speaking either of music or of
very unpretentious and human matters. Conductors as well as ordinary mortals indulge in these
asides, which sometimes are revealing, and which
may here and there provide, through a chance remark, something illuminating about an art not to
be discovered in critical essays, histories, or dic-
tionaries. Mrs. Armsby could claim much. She has
claimed nothing. She lets her guests talk, and describes the scene. The accomplishment back of
this, the results for social development and culture
in her neighborhood—these things, she doubtless
would say, could be left to the accomplishments of
the orchestra. It can here be added, that it is a pity
a similar degree of wisdom and constructive force
could not have been applied to many other musical
institutions. Here, at any rate, is one which has

become a nucleus of artistic effort and growth, of lasting value to its public and hence to the collective musical activity of the nation.

OLIN DOWNES

CONTENTS

xi

xii CONTENTS

ILLUSTRATIONS

I

GABRILOWITSCH ARRIVES

IT was mid-June of 1926. In a corridor, forming one of the promenades of San Francisco's great ferry building, a photographer with a large camera was making squinting calculations through his lens.

"That looks fine, Charlie," commented a news reporter who lounged against a concrete wall near by. "You can get a group by the tower; it makes a good background."

"The sun is too strong there," muttered Charlie from under the folds of black cloth.

"What do you think about it?" queried the reporter turning abruptly to me.

"Ask Fried," I suggested: "the San Francisco *Chronicle* is to run the pictures in Fried's column. There he is now, coming through that archway."

"Good morning, everybody," Fried's throaty voice boomed in a greeting above the babel in the streets.

Redfern Mason, the *Examiner's* forceful music

1

critic, responded with a mild "Hello! I suppose you are here like the rest of us to meet the Gabrilowitsch family."

"That's the intention," returned Fried, "and I see that all of my confrères in music have the same idea. It looks like a convention." Fried waved his hand towards Marie Davidson, Alfred Metzger, Lillian Birmingham, and Joseph Thompson, who were emerging from the caves of small merchandise that lined the depot arcade. Then his reporter's hawk-like eyes pinned themselves on me:

"Going to have any parrots at Gabrilowitsch's concert?" he asked nonchalantly.

"Heaven forbid!" gasped Alfred Metzger.

"Parrots? What do you mean?" Lillian Birmingham's question struggled with the din from a pair of iron girders scraping upon the side wall of a building in process of construction across the way.

"We can't hear anything with that drilling going on. Wait a minute, Alfred, before you tell your story," exclaimed Joe Thompson.

Undaunted, Metzger made a funnel with his hands into which he shouted: "I was speaking of a parrot that came to Sokoloff's concert last Sunday afternoon at Hillsborough." The riveting machine suddenly was silenced by a whistle blowing as two men with a blue map went into conference over the dangling steel beams.

"Go on now," urged Joe Thompson in a tone purposely bland to offset the reverberating whang that pulsated through the ferry building's dome.

"The parrot," Metzger explained, "was a big green-blue-yellow macaw. It rushed like a comet into the concert grounds. A pair of huge red wings brought it out of nowhere to light in a poplar tree just by the stage."

"Dear me! How exciting!" whispered Lillian Birmingham nervously.

"But it was a gorgeous sight with the sun shining on the bird's brilliant colors," exclaimed Marie Davidson.

"Gorgeous, all right," assented Metzger, "but for twenty minutes two thousand people sat like frozen corpses wondering what would happen."

"Well, did he say, 'Polly wants a cracker'? Or did he treat you to a sailor's chanty?"

"Metzger tossed his head ignoring the question. "Everyone," he went on, "wanted to jump out of their seats and shoo the bird away, but what can you do to a parrot that is swinging far up in a poplar tree?"

"Not much," Lillian Birmingham replied readily.

"Fortunately the drums began to beat and the trumpets blared out in a climax so that we all breathed again, for the orchestra was making so much noise that if the bird decided to give us profanity no one would be able to hear it."

"And did you notice that the parrot was the first on the grounds to get away?" asked Marie Davidson with a vague gesture that resembled flight. "When the music stopped he just opened his wings and glided off through the tree-tops."

"Would that some power would make getting home as easy for the rest of us!" Fried exclaimed wistfully. "It is dreadful to have to get out of the crowds and hurry my copy to the office. Now if I only were like the parrot I could be at my desk in a few moments and my disposition would have a chance to become perfect."

"Bruno Walter says," suggested Joe Thompson, "that many of the people in Germany never travel any place except in planes. Why don't *you* try flying down to the country concerts, Alexander?"

Further discussion was prevented by the advance of a porter's truck which clattered out from the shadows that formed a background for the rest-less throngs.

"There is Mr. Gabrilowitsch now," called out Charlie excitedly from his post at the camera; "don't let him get away and don't forget that I am standing here waiting to photograph him."

My eyes traveled after the newspaper men who trooped towards some approaching figures and I saw Gabrilowitsch pointing out his luggage to Haidee Pohlman, our secretary. After a moment of inspection I stepped forward to claim my prize. Someone touched Gabrilowitsch on the arm and gave him my name. With a quick gesture and a warm smile he turned and bowed. In the next second he spoke eagerly to a small, dark-haired woman standing close to him:

"Clara," he urged, "come and meet Mrs. Armsby."

Gabrilowitsch had been described as aloof, pre-ferring to be in the society of his family and in-timates rather than that of strangers; but I found myself basking in his friendliness and attracted by his persuasive voice which made everything that he said seem worth listening to. Mrs. Gabrilo-witsch, looking delicate and feminine, nodded towards a young woman:

"This is Nina, our daughter," she explained smilingly.

"They tell me we must pose for photographs," remarked Gabrilowitsch in a matter-of-fact way. "Come on then, please," he urged while he managed to gather us into a cluster about him.

To the reporters who clamored for interviews Gabrilowitsch called out over his shoulder, as laden with hand luggage we walked to the motor:

"Not now—come down soon to Hillsborough."

The chauffeur turned the nose of the car towards the peninsula, steering us skillfully through the criss-cross streets of San Francisco's water front and passing close to the big white Orient-bound steamships lying at anchor in the harbor. Amazed at the crown of hills that top the city's heights and offer acreage for hundreds of homes Gabrilowitsch called his wife's attention to them:

"Look, Clara, at all those cliffs. Do you mean to say," he asked turning to me, "that motors go up and down such steep places?" and pointing to a perpendicular street he shuddered lightly as he added: "Not for me—I wouldn't like that!"

Amused at his concern, I told him that we were used to clinging to and crawling along the slopes and I repeated the pet phrase of a friend—always used as we zigzagged downward: 'Well, here goes nothing!'

Gabrilowitsch changed abruptly to another subject:

"Now that I have a chance to ask you I want to know how you happened to send for me?"

"Because I have always had a great admiration for your work."

"This is interesting," Gabrilowitsch went on in his bantering manner. "Where did you hear me conduct an orchestra? Have you been to Detroit?"

"Oh, no; my introduction to your conducting was made years ago in New York. I particularly remember one all-Russian program that was thrilling."

"So that is how I happen to be here. If you liked my work why did you not come back of the stage and tell me so?"

"Too shy," I admitted.

While listening to this light conversation, I had a chance to watch the changing moods which made Mrs. Gabrilowitsch's face interesting and fascinating. My mind reverted to a little white church in a small Illinois town where I had heard her father,

Mark Twain, give one of his witty talks. I had then been stirred by the brilliancy of almond-shaped eyes in Mark Twain's shaggy, lion-like head, and now looking at me, from under the creamy white brow of his daughter, were eyes that were also beautiful with an odd and exotic mystery in their depths.

The value of Mark Twain to the world has not been allowed to diminish or to recede into the background, by his famous son-in-law and his family. Clara Gabrilowitsch is asked often to give her intimate pictures of the humorist before women's clubs and literary societies and many references to the humorist color Gabrilowitsch's anecdotes.

The impressions conveyed by the Gabrilowitsches are best described as romantic. Those large picture hats, the soft fluffy feminine chiffons that Clara Clemens Gabrilowitsch delights in, and the nineteenth-century picturesqueness of Gabrilowitsch, which is accentuated by the high white collars, are reminiscent of the days of neckerchiefs and proclaim allegiance to Schumann, Schubert, and Romanticism.

The modish dress and manners of her contemporaries seemed in harsh contrast to the gentle poetic moods evoked by the gauze draperies and soft laces of Mark Twain's daughter. The glamorous aura of these two personalities made fervid the tide of public interest that stirred through the country at the time of the courtship and marriage of the Russian pianist and his American bride.

From New York Gabrilowitsch moved to Detroit, where, in his position as Director of the Symphony, he dominates the musical thought of that city. Tours with his orchestra, piano recitals through America and Europe, identified him as an international artist and the audiences of two continents clamored for opportunities to hear performances in which his genius was displayed in its dual rôle.

Such were my thoughts as the motor traveled over the broad highway which paralleled the dark green waters of the bay and the hills of the Oakland side, whose curving lines swept over the open spaces of the sky like a flock of blue pigeons flying southward through terraces of white clouds.

We crawled past huge oil tanks fastened on to powerful trucks. The rumble of machinery at work in repairing the concrete roads and the clap of hammers descending on rock piles shook the car although it was in motion.

Clusters of deep orange California poppies shone

from the lowlands undimmed by dreariness and dust. During intervals free from noise I related briefly the origin and purpose of the Philharmonic Society, and the Gabrilowitsches were deeply interested and wanted to know all about this new project for the promotion of Symphony Concerts.

The adventure, I explained, was the outcome of a visit made by Mrs. John Casserly to the Hollywood Bowl. Stirred by the open air music which she had heard in the great amphitheatre Mrs. Casserly returned home with a plan to launch a similar series of concerts in Hillsborough. Alfred Metzger, editor of the *Musical Courier,* also dreamed of getting such an enterprise under way in San Francisco and he communicated his ideas by letter to Mrs. Casserly, advising her that the San Francisco personnel would be available and that guest conductors could be offered engagements in both San Francisco and San Mateo. Working swiftly, Mrs. Casserly at once organized her society and announced her plans. San Francisco when asked for a list of possible leaders was surprised to learn that preparations for the country series were so advanced and explained that as far as the city was concerned all projects were still unformed. Lack of funds was holding San Francisco from making offers to the orchestra and it was feared that the members of the Symphony might seek summer engagements in other localities. Mrs. Casserly, who was financing her plans without outside assistance, volunteered to aid also in San Francisco and whenever it was necessary assured artists by an advance payment on their contracts that their engagements were protected.

"It is splendid," commented Gabrilowitsch enthusiastically, "but whom did you finally secure for conductors?"

"Nikolai Sokoloff, Henry Hadley, Alfred Hertz, and yourself," was my reply.

"Have you a theatre?" Gabrilowitsch asked.

"Only a makeshift one, located on the Hillsborough School grounds, with a crude stage and a canvas covering."

I felt some misgivings as I described the meagre equipment which would soon have to bear the professional sizing up that Gabrilowitsch would give it. My discomfort did not lessen as I continued excusing our lack of a proper theatre.

"But you must have some kind of a shell to project the sound," protested Gabrilowitsch.

"We have, but I want you to be prepared to discount all of the crudities; for our stage looks about like the little booth in which Pagliacci kills Nedda."

"Heavens!" laughed Gabrilowitsch. "So you expect me to conduct symphonies in a children's playground from a toy platform?"

"Please remember that we are just experimenting," I pleaded.

"We are to stay at the house of a friend of yours, you said in your letter," interrupted Clara Gabrilowitsch, and she asked eagerly for details of the home in which her family was to visit.

"Mr. and Mrs. Samuel Knight, who live on the hill only a little way from me, have invited you to be their guest throughout your stay in California. The place is equipped with servants and a motor, and you only have to unpack your trunks and prepare to enjoy their beautiful gardens."

"It is the kindest and most generous invitation we have ever received. How can we thank such wonderful people?"

Whether tramping over country lanes, or through San Francisco streets that were ghostly with swirling fogs, Gabrilowitsch, true to an instinctive liking for summer dress, wore spotless white and ignored the custom of appearing in a hat.

"I am always happier in white," was his explanation, "and I wear it whenever I can. Perhaps I follow the taste of Mark Twain, who never wanted to wear colors, feeling that in white he was at his best."

The high collar, which furnished the key-note to Gabrilowitsch's personal taste in dress, was not discarded with the informal attire, and the ceremonious four or five inches of starched linen, stiffly hugging the artist's throat, seemed inharmonious. What unexpectedly prompted the change to a sport shirt and soft collar was a mystery, for upon a certain concert day, Gabrilowitsch, stepping down the stairway ready to leave for the theatre, seemed longer than usual in getting together his music and glancing over the contents of his brief-case. Three o'clock was near and I stood anxiously waiting for my star to give the word that we could be on our way. What was keeping us? I wondered. With that trick of lifting his eyebrow quizzically Gabrilowitsch looked at me shyly as he said:

"You haven't noticed my soft collar."

I did not know just how to reply.

"I am wearing it in order to be like my new

friends and to fit into their world," was the simple explanation.

Studying scores filled Gabrilowitsch's leisure hours; the work of memorizing and practising the piano went on with but little interruption or relaxation. At five o'clock critics and friends were asked into the Knight garden for a cup of tea. Gabrilowitsch was to be found with his books out in the covered swinging couch and here he could be drawn into talking of music and composers.

"Composers should have permanent control of their work," he asserted, "for they have as much right to the material they create as they have to any property which they may own."

"Jazz," Gabrilowitsch declared, "has its own field but the practice of taking themes from classical music is unethical; as for modern music, the greater part of it will not survive."

A merciless sun in a cloudless sky burned everyone and everything to a crisp on the day of Gabrilowitsch's first concert. The uncovered seats in the school grounds had no protection from the glare and patrons finally moved their chairs from the open field close to the low hanging eaves of the Spanish school buildings. In the shadows thrown by the tile roofs there was some relief from the sicken-

*To my dear friend Leonora
with love and
admiration

Ossip
August
1933*

Ossip Gabrilowitsch

ing heat. Only loyalty to the music and to the adventure which the concerts represented persuaded the public to submit to the discomfort that strained even the most tolerant dispositions. There were moments when the audience moved in such numbers towards cooler locations that it looked as if Gabrilowitsch, like St. Francis, might be left playing only to the birds; but the crowd did not go farther away than the trees near by, for they were intent upon the new way of directing without a score and upon Gabrilowitsch's gestures, which controlled the orchestra with a freedom only possible when there is no printed page before the leader.

Through a sensibility that is recognized as the exclusive possession of poets, music was set before Californians in a new and appealing manner.

Twilight was obscuring the white curve of the young moon as we left the concert grounds. Beyond the skyline played the echo of Siegfried's horn; its full-blown song must have alarmed the furry creatures of the hills. A heavy odor from the musk of bay trees sweetened the advancing dusk.

II

HENRY HADLEY CARRIES ON THE CONCERTS

"Music is not my forte but I can see what a wonderful power it has for bringing people closer together. Take the Grove play for example: I feel sure that most of those men who meet there for the 'Jinks' don't know any more about a symphony than I do, but as they lounge about the camp fire on Sunday nights and listen to the orchestra there isn't one of them that is left unmoved."

A Bohemian Club member who had dropped in at the Curran Theatre when the orchestra was rehearsing had engaged the first 'cellist in conversation and he continued talking as the orchestra piped out in shrill little runs during the tuning-up process. The 'cellist, glad to gossip for a few moments before the tedious grilling over the Brahms C minor, commenced interrogating the visitor:

"Our present guest conductor, Dr. Henry Hadley, is a leading spirit in your club, is he not?"

"Did you ever hear his *Atonement of Pan,* for which Joe Redding wrote the words? We have never given a better work."

"I was at the matinée when the *Pan* music was repeated for the public in the old Tivoli Opera House," recalled the 'cellist.

"What did you think of it?" asked the Bohemian.

"It was superbly pagan and I can imagine the Greeks must have had such a Chorus for their feasts to Bacchus or Apollo."

"That is Henry's idea of it, too, I imagine," mused the Bohemian. "I wonder," he continued, "what his *Angelus* will be like; you know he is to play it at his concert in Woodland Theatre next Sunday."

"Here is Hadley now; ask him about it."

With languid grace, and manner a trifle diffident, Hadley passed through the big door leading into the hall. In his physical make-up something delicate, almost frail, subtly revealed the romantic dreamer and the artist.

Fair-haired, angelic-faced Louis Persinger, our concert-master, stopped the conductor for a moment and the voluble clubman resumed his chatter.

"Hadley was in San Francisco as director of the Symphony for several years in and about 1911; that was before he was made associate director of the Philharmonic of New York."

"You are right," replied the 'cellist; "I was playing in the orchestra at that time."

"Look at Henry," urged the Bohemian; "he is very little different now, a bit older and a trifle more serious perhaps, but the same good fellow." Warm affection glowed in the voice that summed up the changes in the Hadley that was returning to us.

"How dramatic and picturesque he was in the old days as he stepped out on the stage dressed in his dark morning suit and puffed black silk tie with the bunch of Russian violets in his button-hole. I always enjoyed," the clubman observed ironically, "watching the lovely ladies sweep into the stage boxes before Henry's concert and seeing them regard one another inquisitively through half-closed eyes as the sardonic *Don Juan* boasted of his amorous conquests in the Strauss tone poem. I often wondered what thoughts floated back of the calm expressions in those beautiful faces."

"You had better go slow now, old man," warned the 'cellist; "here comes our leader."

"What are you good people whispering about?"

Hadley asked with a bright laugh. "You all look so serious."

"We are talking about you, of course, Henry," volunteered his friend.

"That is a useless topic," remonstrated the Director. He swept back the long plume of blond hair from his high white forehead while a smile deepened the drooping lines on either side of his expressive mouth. "Talk about my music; it is a more worth-while subject," was the crisp comment.

"Tell us about your *Angelus*," requested the Bohemian.

Hadley jerked his head quickly to one side of his high collar. "My *Angelus*," he answered glowingly, "is from my Third Symphony; you will like it and it will be suitable for California, as this country is much like the lovely part of Italy where I wrote the music. I lived in a little village near Milan while I worked on the score in the summer of 1906. I felt that I had found an ideal place for work in the sheltered grove of a forest close to the town. I noticed each afternoon the sound of bells that was wafted to me across the fields from a far-away church and it seemed to me that I could use the theme that I heard in my symphony, so I jotted

down the song of the chimes and made their hymn
the subject of the second part of the work. I call
this movement *The Angelus.*"

"What other numbers will you play on Sunday
afternoon, Henry? I hope *Don Juan.*"

Hadley and the Bohemian looked at one another with a contagious humor that overflowed into
outspoken thoughts.

"Do you remember the storm of discussion that
arose when you first played the Strauss work?"
asked the Bohemian.

"People were terribly agitated, weren't they?"
remarked Hadley good-humoredly. "I never shall
forget it; they did not know what to think.
Strange," he added thoughtfully, "how quickly
we adapt ourselves to new ideas after we have become familiar with them; for now *Don Juan* is
quite acceptable even to the most squeamish taste."

"Yes," replied the 'cellist," and it also interests
me to observe how often music is influenced by the
dominant forces that shape the era in which it is
written. There is Beethoven's *Eroica,* inspired by
the composer's wish to pay tribute to Napoleon.
In our times the power of the machine is exalted by
Honneger in his *Pacific 231* and John Alden Car-

penter in *Skyscrapers*. So many of the modern works are written to symbolize the materialistic tendencies of our age."

"What we need most," Hadley replied thoughtfully, "is the opportunity to hear our own composers. It is very difficult to get Americans placed on symphony programs, and at one time I raised a special fund to produce compositions which were otherwise fated to be shelved and forgotten although they were of a nature that well deserved recognition. Students of real ability have told me that they are abandoning music as a profession since it is impossible to get conductors interested enough to try out their scores. Naturally we cannot develop talent in our own composers as long as conditions such as these smother all attempts at progress. I hope some day to see compositions of Americans replacing the works of some of their contemporaries from other countries, whose pieces are played in America because foreign leaders insist upon preventing them."

"What can be done about it?" Hadley was asked.

"I don't know, for conductors come here from abroad and play nothing but European compositions; of course a few composers like Gruenberg and Deems Taylor are heard and I can't complain of being ignored; but what about many of the other composers?"

"Can't this state of affairs be remedied?" wondered the 'cellist.

"It could be if Americans would insist upon it," Hadley responded warmly. "What is the first thing that happens to me when I go to England to conduct?"

"Tell me," urged the listener.

"I am visited immediately by a gentleman who asks me how long I am to stay and what I am going to play. When I ask him why he wants to know, the answer is: 'Because it is our business to protect our artists.' "

"That is a great idea," commented the 'cellist fervently.

"The same thing happens to me when I go to the Argentine; I am told that I must place at least one piece by an Argentine composer on each program, but are European conductors ever given such an order by Americans? No, indeed!"

"I cannot talk more about my crusade in this direction now," Hadley said regretfully, "for it is time to commence rehearsing."

Peeling off his coat the Director ran lightly up

the steps to the stage. With his classic profile turned towards us in the dim light of the drab room he nodded to the orchestra, giving the first command in a voice which held in it something of the treble sweetness of the boy chorister.

The opening phrases of the Brahms C minor moved out from the taut skins of the drums to prowl unleashed through the exits, on into the secret alleyways that hugged the walls of the theatre. Here the clusters of sound dispersed, some of them to stray into the chop suey restaurants and the rathskellars of the crooked passage-way below; others lived to reach the open sky, to float with the pale clouds until they were overtaken and silenced by the mighty clang of the city's voices.

III

ALFRED HERTZ

The San Francisco Symphony Orchestra is largely the product of the executive and artistic ability of Alfred Hertz, since he selected and trained much of its personnel in the art of ensemble playing.

The Hertz villa at Sea Cliff shows the rugged and independent spirit which shapes the ideas of this interpreter of mighty symphonies. In the home out upon the cliffs overlooking San Francisco Bay are projecting windows through which can be seen the wild crags and the mountains where waves surge over giant rocks, as fiercely possessive in their savage embraces as the flames which defended the couch of Brünnhilde.

Over the hospitality offered in this ménage presides Mrs. Hertz, who is best known to the coterie of musicians who cluster about at her supper parties as "Lily." Topics dearest to the soul of Lily Hertz are her little mountain cabin and the unflagging care which she gives her health and her beloved Alfred.

"We live only once," she says, "and we are here such a short time, why not be free and why do the tiresome things which bring us no happiness?"

In order to secure "health and happiness" for her husband, Mrs. Hertz hovers over him with a solicitous desire to check in him any indiscretion which may interrupt these blessings.

"No coffee this noon, Alfred dear," rings across the table in a wifely tone.

Alfred hears the warning as his arm is out-stretched towards the big white and gold cup at his place. He breathes the fragrance escaping from the coffee pot in the hand of the servant. Smiling wistfully he murmurs:

"Can't I have one cup?"

"No, Alfred," says Mrs. Hertz in a tone of final-ity.

"Oh! Mrs. Hertz," interrupts a guest at the family luncheon, "don't be cruel; let him have his coffee."

Slowly and meditatively the vivacious hostess reconsiders the order to her submissive husband and reluctantly she gives way to the importuning guest while she shakes all of the tiny curls that cluster upon her head like hundreds of petals on a silver flower.

"I will give in since you urge it," she concludes.

Alfred's smile broadens and he throws back his bearded head to inhale the rings of smoke curling from a black cigar. Soon he is sipping his golden brown coffee.

In this atmosphere of comfort it is not difficult to coax him to the piano, although he protests that he is no pianist.

"Just give us a little something from *Tristan*," wheedles an admirer.

After a few *arpeggios* the greatest of love songs steals through the studio. While listening one remembers the operatic triumphs of Hertz and his genius for Wagnerian productions which gave him fame in Germany and later placed him in a prominent position at the Metropolitan.

Hertz is known extensively as the Father of the Hollywood Bowl. The scheme for using this natural amphitheatre in the hills close to Hollywood developed slowly into the present setting for the superb symphonies under the stars. In the beginning of the project no leader could be found who would accept the invitation to conduct in the crude space which, in its simplicity, resembled arrangements for a large camp-fire gathering. Hertz was able to subordinate his important position in music to the vision which he foresaw in the idea of the Bowl, and he alone from among a number of symphony leaders who were invited to give concerts was willing to submit to the inconveniences and informalities of the rustic open-air theatre.

In July of 1921 with only the night sky for a dome the Los Angeles Symphony Orchestra under Hertz played to thousands in the canyon that forms the site of the present great Bowl. Now artists clamor for a chance to appear in the internationally famous amphitheatre; but no matter how numerous may be the stellar attractions upon the gigantic Hollywood stage "Papa Hertz" has his series of performances wherein the hills resound with a tribute of cheering in affectionate acknowledgment of his first services in the interests of open-air symphony music in California.

IV

BRUNO WALTER CONDUCTS IN THE
NEW WOODLAND THEATRE

THE idea of summer concerts pleased the neighborhood, and community enthusiasm was expressed by
a vote of its citizens to build a theatre in the creek-
bed back of the Hillsborough School grounds. This
hollow at the foot of the sloping hillside offered
some protection against wind, lying, as it does, in
a natural cup of the earth. The stage would have
to stand upon the west rim of the ravine. Templeton Crocker, who owned this section of land, generously consented to our use of the broad knoll
which was to hold our shell.

Nikolai Sokoloff led the first performance in the
Woodland Theatre. Sokoloff had collected much
fresh material for his programs. Such numbers as
Loeffler's *Pagan Poem,* Douglas Moore's *P. T. Bar-
num,* and Bloch's symphony *Israel* were in his interesting repertoire. These unfamiliar works engaged the attention of the orchestra for many

weeks, and often in order to achieve some degree of perfection extra rehearsals were required.

Ossip Gabrilowitsch shared honors with Nikolai Sokoloff in conducting the first concerts given in the New Theatre. Bruno Walter was the additional artist who came to us from the Hollywood Bowl for a pair of concerts.

On the morning of Walter's first rehearsal he hurried to the Auditorium directly from the train. After a reading of Tchaikovsky's *Romeo and Juliet* the leader asked for Schreker's *Birthday of the Infanta*. In a casual voice he remarked: "The serenade calls for a guitar; I presume that you have one for this part."

No, we did not have a guitar, as the Schreker score was new to us and Walter had brought the music with him so that there had been no time for preliminary checking-up. Our orchestra manager hurried away to search for a guitarist. In the meanwhile we played through Wagner's Fire music. Out from some corner of San Francisco's Little Italy and into the great auditorium was hurried a small dark-browed man who came scrambling along, through the echoing building, after Walter Oesterreicher. Bruno Walter regarded the dazed-looking Italian doubtfully, then directed him to a seat close to the second violins. From here he was to thrum out the serenade. Spectators craned their necks, agog with curiosity, and the Schreker composition was soon under way. Walter, with precise beat, cued in the guitarist, who missed his signal. Walter, unperturbed, began again. Attempt after attempt was made to induce Little Italy to approach, if possible, the pace of the other players, but his phrasing smacked of gondola days, and its drifting spirit, tinged with long rhapsodic pauses upon sustained notes, bewildered the orchestra. Walter at last dismissed the olive-skinned troubadour, assigning his song to the strings, and the serenade flowed out minus the realism of the guitar.

Concert dates for Walter and Gabrilowitsch overlapped, making it possible for the two friends to visit and to drive about the country together.

Gabrilowitsch entertained at a small dinner at Pierre's French Restaurant before Walter's concert in San Francisco. Crab *à la Pierre* and a sugary dessert of baked fruits, covered with an amber-colored syrup that tasted like thick honey, were the dishes especially selected and prepared by Pierre. As these masterpieces came to the table the little Frenchman watched eagerly to see how they were received while he twirled his mustaches in the fierce and gallant manner of the Latin who knows he is unrivalled. Pierre assured us that the sauces had been mixed by his own hand.

"Do you cook much yourself?" asked Mrs. Gabrilowitsch.

"Not so much in winter, but in the summer time, when I take my family off on a camping trip into the high Sierras, then I am chef. I have a big motor which is fitted up as a traveling kitchen and light-housekeeping van. My daughter drives and we go over all of the most beautiful country in the high mountains seeking a place that pleases us; then we make our camp. Neighboring campers smell my fire and the good things cooking and frequently they find an excuse to come over asking for some small favor. Of course I invite them to try my fresh fish cooked *à la Pierre.*"

The eyes of the *restaurateur* grew dreamy with recollection and in homage to the mountain trout he blew a kiss into the air from his expressive finger tips.

"Are they as delicious as all that?" queried Mrs. Gabrilowitsch, who was enjoying Pierre's dramatic descriptions.

"*Mais oui; tout ce qu'il y a de bon!*" he assured her.

From the low-ceilinged narrow room, which was becoming smoke-filled by the cigarettes of late diners, we motored to the big Civic Auditorium. The *Rienzi* Overture stood first on Walter's program. Gabrilowitsch, settling back in one of the stiff chairs, sighed luxuriously as the music began.

"I am thinking how good it is to be sitting here listening to some other poor fellow who has to be up there doing the work," he whispered.

"What a noble theme the *Rienzi* really is when we hear it played as it is to-night!" commented Gabrilowitsch after the first number. "What have we next? Oh! yes, the Schreker."

The dancing themes of this number, which related the moving story of the little Infanta and her playmates, fluttered forth lightly in ballet style leading up to the scene in which the dwarf, dazzled by the idea that he has charmed the Princess and her ladies-in-waiting, is suddenly confronted by his grotesque figure in the mirror. The music swells here savagely while the mountebank utters his broken cries. Reminiscent of John Alden Carpenter's work on the same subject, the Schreker is not so imaginative a representation.

Through the externals of Walter's art could be

sensed his knowledge of opera. While listening to his interpretation one felt that flesh-and-blood story-tellers were setting forth their passions and their purposes through the medium of music.

V

GABRILOWITSCH REHEARSES

"Everybody works but Father." Gabrilowitsch threw down his baton and the orchestra moved uneasily in their chairs.

It was Wednesday morning. Rehearsals had commenced with Gabrilowitsch again leading. Who was guilty? None other than the incomparable first violin section with Piastro in command. In the brass and woodwind choirs there was joy, for usually the reproofs fell their way.

"Now we will begin once more, please," continued Gabrilowitsch from the high perch where his coatless figure balancing neatly on the long-legged stool swayed gracefully with his precise and delicate counting.

"Four bars before L and *you*"—Gabrilowitsch pointed to the 'cellos and oboes—"make your notes shorter."

The music was under way once again. Debussy's mystic tone picture, *The Clouds* billowed forth with the violins subdued by their mutes. Once more Gabrilowitsch dropped his stick and this time he smiled faintly as he commented:

"Yes! It's a lovely sound BUT—"

Pausing thoughtfully for a moment Gabrilowitsch waited to see if his criticism would be effective without further explanation. The orchestra was quick to get his meaning and the lackadaisical quality disappeared from the music while Piastro shoved his chin savagely into his fiddle, sending out a tone of astonishing beauty.

Suddenly into the dull and commonplace surroundings shot a strange grating and swishing noise. The odd sound was finally identified as a mop gurgling on its way from a bucket to the floor of the Auditorium. A stooped figure with a bundle of rags tied on to a long stick was cleaning up. The pale suds swirled foamingly through the rows of empty seats and as I looked it seemed apparent that the moppist was whistling a gay little tune. The orchestra had heard, but true to their discipline played on.

What had happened to Gabrilowitsch? Could it be that the famous ear which could stop a rehearsal to call out to a clarinet "Not B flat but C natural" was not disturbed by the feet of the cleaner as he dragged along through the trail of frothing water?

I found myself whispering, "Gabrilowitsch! Gabrilowitsch! What is the matter?" Whole tone melodies of Debussy fought for place against the tune warbled by the laborer.

At last our conductor checked the orchestra; then he deliberately and dispassionately removed his spectacles before speaking. Turning to face the immense hall he spied the white-coated workman at his toil.

"My good man," called out Gabrilowitsch, "please listen to me. Either you or I stop work and it doesn't make a bit of difference to me which one of us goes."

Someone in the back of the auditorium nudged the "white-wings," repeating to him what Gabrilowitsch had just finished saying. The figure in the conductor's stand stood quietly waiting for a decision. There was no anger, no scene; just an icy composure which made Gabrilowitsch as remote from our vulgar atmosphere as a lofty Himalayan peak.

"Oh! Does he mean me?" jerked out the workman.

"Yes, he certainly does," explained Tom Girton, who had been dragged out from the manager's office to enforce discipline.

"Oh!" repeated the culprit.

"Don't say another word," warned Girton, "but beat it, do you hear? Beat it!"

Bump! bump! clanged the iron pail against the exit door.

"Please," remarked Gabrilowitsch calmly, "page two, four measures before L."

VI

OUR SOCIETY IS DISRUPTED

ALTHOUGH our guest leaders had aided the Philharmonic to achieve distinction, there was another angle to the Society's affairs which was not so fortunate. Financially we had not succeeded as we had expected and at the close of the 1927 season our difficulties were discussed by the executive committee.

Different viewpoints over policies divided the board into factions. A study of the concert charts showed that if one conductor appeared for more than two or three concerts in a season our audiences and our receipts both dwindled. Extra rehearsals for some of the more elaborate programs absorbed large sums of money, noticeably increasing the deficit. Prophecies of disaster to the Philharmonic were whirling about the neighborhood and our friends besieged us with advice and suggestions for safeguarding our future.

A few of the officers actively engaged in promoting the concerts understood that it would be nec-

essary to continue with the original program of
visiting leaders to conduct our summer series. We
felt also that further developments necessitated our
securing the coöperation of the San Francisco Summer Symphony Association. If they would pool
their rehearsals with ours and would give the same
symphony at their Tuesday concert that we used on
Sunday afternoon, we might be assured of a smooth
performance and we could avoid the extra rehearsals which played havoc with our cost of production.
Interesting the Hollywood Bowl to affiliate themselves with us was also suggested as a way of attracting desirable artists to California.

Some of our supporters were opposed to this plan
and felt that our only concern should be to give
fresh numbers on our programs. This could be
achieved by searching for and presenting new music and perhaps also by giving some ballets and
tone-dramas. If this were done we would have to
raise an additional twenty thousand dollars a season, and it would be advisable to use only one
leader who could drill the orchestra and teach them
to play in his manner.

This vision of the scope of our mission was very
progressive, exciting and interesting, but in our
humble place, as beginners in a new musical en-

terprise, we could only hope to move as fast as our public could or would keep pace with us, and much modern music, and the playing of works which were unfamiliar, had already proved unsatisfactory to the majority of our patrons. Since we were now backed by guarantors and could not depend alone upon one generous private purse, as we had done in the first year, we must meet the desires of our public if we were to continue to exist.

Should Hollywood and San Francisco combine with us we could assure a guest leader engagements with the three associations, which would warrant his coming upon the long journey from Europe or the East. A few committee members of our board approved this plan but those opposing it were in the majority.

Being convinced that our only chance of becoming a permanent institution rested upon putting into operation the policies which included a close affiliation between ourselves and the other two summer symphony organizations in California, I had no other choice than to hand in my resignation as president of the Philharmonic, which would leave the way clear for those who thought that they could find a better way of conducting our affairs.

In the weeks following my retirement from the

Philharmonic I found recreation and diversion in New York where the concerts and theatres engrossed me with their display of talent and their excellent presentation of their material. While I was enjoying the treasures that the arts were furnishing for their devotees a telegram arrived from Charles Blyth saying that he had been elected president of the Philharmonic and urging me to take the chairmanship of the Music Committee.

Here was a chance to put into action our co-operative plan and, after long distance telephoning with Charles Blyth, our new régime was under way. It was a fortunate circumstance that Allan Balch, president of the Hollywood Bowl, and Raymond Brite, the Bowl manager, were in New York for the purpose of engaging leaders for the coming summer just at the time that I needed to confer with them with regard to the uniting of our forces for the mutual benefit of our musical associations.

After conversations with the Hollywood officials it was agreed that I should do the negotiating in New York towards the 1928 season.

VII

AGAIN GABRILOWITSCH

It was to Gabrilowitsch that I again looked first for assistance. A telegram sent to him to Detroit brought an immediate answer.

"Will be in New York next week. Can you take lunch with me on Thursday?"

In the restaurant of the Savoy-Plaza we met to discuss the important details of his return to California.

"We want you for three concerts, Ossip," I urged in the first breathing space after we were seated at one of the little tables. "You will not disappoint me, will you?"

Gabrilowitsch looked at me; then grew thoughtful. He did not answer immediately and my mind began to whirl and to anticipate that he might possibly refuse the offer although in a recent letter he had promised that he would accept an engagement. I had to gain his consent:

"You must come, Ossip," I pleaded. "I have to

run this thing myself and if I can't have you I'm afraid I shall fail."

He smiled with that slow, almost lazy smile of his; then jumped into speech:

"But you don't give me any vacation and I need a rest. I should go over to Europe and give a few concerts and then take a holiday."

"You can do that next year," I interrupted. "You must come to us this summer," I begged. "Come just this year and then, if you feel that it is too much of a sacrifice and too fatiguing, we won't insist that you return again unless you really want to."

Gabrilowitsch was silent while he turned over in his mind what I had said to him.

Suddenly he looked at me and irrelevantly exclaimed:

"See that man at the table just back of you a little to your left?"

I turned my head to get a view of our neighbor and observed a very impressive-looking person with thoughtful brown eyes and a patriarchal head.

"That is Gatti-Casazza," Gabrilowitsch whispered.

The impresario of the Metropolitan held our attention and my nerves thrilled as I remembered

Farrar, Jeritza, Bori, Caruso, Tibbett—singers who
have charmed the patrons that nightly throng into
the wine-red curving tiers of seats and boxes that
surround the stage of the great opera house. I remembered the gorgeous, unforgettable voice of
Caruso singing in *Pagliacci,* and the tenderness of
Bori's Juliet.

Perhaps Gatti-Casazza heard some of these things
too, for he sat on after his repast, with his head
bowed in a reverie, glancing frequently at his quiet
hands as if asking them questions. What was it
that held the man in so prolonged a musing? My
curiosity was sharpened as the moments went by
but I heard Gabrilowitsch speaking:

"As I was saying," he emphasized, "we will need
extra brasses for the *Valkyrie.*"

I turned again to busy myself with the work
which was ahead of us. The little tables of the café
—with their white damask, their silver service and
elaborately crested china—were jumbled together
curiously in my mind because of my anxiety about
the future of the Philharmonic and the difficulties
that faced us.

Our new project seemed like a very small and
timid David that was setting forth to kill the giant
of apathy and indifference that had commenced to

crush the enthusiasm of many of our former ad-
vocates. I would have liked to talk with Gatti-
Casazza who was sitting so close to me and who
knew well the difficulties encountered in problems
such as mine. Still intent upon his thoughts he had
been joined by an obsequious, earnest little man
with a sheep-like face and beseeching eyes. Evidently the newcomer was asking a favor, for Gatti-
Casazza frowned, then smiled, then shook his head
in the negative.

Gabrilowitsch spoke again:

"We will do the Scriabin *Divine Poem;* it will
take with your audience I am sure. I have a free
hour now," he added, "and if you haven't anything
better to do would you like me to play for you?"

We left the glittering café for my little drawing-
room, where I listened to Schubert and Schumann,
whose gentle moods coaxed me away from the practical side of music.

As Gabrilowitsch played on he banished from
the little room the dull ways of prosaic living and
long after he had gone the walls still trembled with
the bright, alive music. On the piano were clusters
of white lilies which had come to me with a card
that said:

"Not roses for war but lilies for peace." This was

Gabrilowitsch's way of helping me to forget the sad days that had troubled me after my resignation from the Philharmonic. There is a real portrait in this episode; for if you are inclined to be sluggish and contented, or smug and fatuous, Gabrilowitsch goads you with irony and smiling mockery until you are transformed into a veritable dynamo, but if one has been troubled he restores with lilies and Schumann.

VIII

ARTHUR JUDSON OUTLINES HIS PLAN:
MOLINARI'S NEW YORK *PREMIÈRE*

ALBERT COATES and Bernardino Molinari were
being talked of in New York as possible leaders for
summer concerts to be given in that city and in
Philadelphia. It would add to the renown of California could these European celebrities be secured
for appearance in the West. Molinari, who is the
permanent director of the orchestra at the Augusteo in Rome, and who was described as Latin and
fiery, was soon to appear in New York. Should the
Italian live up to his reputation he would be a sen-
sation for Hollywood and Northern California.

Having in mind the commission I was to exe-
cute with regard to the engaging of leaders I made
my first trip to Arthur Judson's office—located in
the Steinway Building on Fifty-seventh Street. The
weighty architecture of this structure well sym-
bolizes the strength and power of the Steinway
name and typifies a business era which has forced

commercial concerns to advertise their importance by costly edifices.

High up in its battlements is housed the Judson Bureau. From this central stronghold artists are "routed" throughout the country to agents in other cities. Impressed by the influence which Judson exerts in all branches of music I was trying to sum up my ideas before approaching him, but the elevator had me in a jiffy deposited at his door.

The "Czar" was seated at his desk when I entered his private office to inquire for guest conductors. Quickly he raised his eyes from the many papers scattered before him and I had a chance to look at his handsome face with its smooth, bronzed contours and keen hazel eyes above which strong, curly, greying hair gave to his head a touch of rugged power. Judson stood to welcome me: his height and heavy physique matched his remarkable head. Greeting me affably while I seated myself he steered the conversation by remarking:

"I hear that you want to talk to me about concerts in California."

I began to tell my story while he made little marks upon a concert schedule which was spread out before him. His thoughts were masked by an indifferent expression and I felt that I was not es-

pecially interesting him until I commenced to outline the plan of working out a combination for
summer concerts which would include not only
the associations in the West but also an alliance
with the New York Stadium and possibly Philadelphia. He looked up quickly with a wide-awake
glance and then spoke with the enthusiasm I had
been waiting for:

"Well, this is something like it. You have a really
constructive scheme here and the New York Stadium will be glad to join you whenever we can
in making combined offerings to conductors."

Exciting days followed as cables were rushed
back and forth to the leaders who were abroad, in
order to find out who among them might be available for summer engagements in America.

In the midst of negotiations Molinari arrived and
gave his first concert at the Metropolitan. This occasion did not offer a fair opportunity for a display of his talent. He had no knowledge of English
and he was leading a strange orchestra, while rehearsals had been insufficient. These handicaps
made Molinari's work seem strained and tedious at
times, but one could feel that under better conditions all that was delicate, careful, and beautiful in
his music would appear to greater advantage.

A day or so after Molinari's *première* Philip Murray, who was managing Molinari, arranged to have the Molinaris, Margherita de Vecchi, and me meet at luncheon. Margherita and I arrived at the Crillon earlier than the rest of the party. We were shaking the first snow of winter from our clothing when the others joined us.

As Molinari walked into the lobby of the restaurant I watched his slight figure approaching. His manner was alert and eager as he asked questions about everything which he had seen since his arrival in America. He was wearing a dark grey, soft felt hat slightly tilted over one eye. This he removed and at the same time he slipped off a green overcoat smartly trimmed with a grey astrachan collar. A charming smile twinkled in his eye and played about his serious mouth. Gallantly he kissed Margherita's hand and mine as the introductions were made.

Following Phil Murray's lead, like leaves trooping on the currents of a driving wind, we swept into the café. The three Italian women in the party were animated, quick-speaking creatures. Madame Molinari smiled frequently and her lovely brown eyes held a beautiful, melting tenderness in their gentle depths. The quick staccato voice of Molinari was like a chisel breaking off phrases from topics of conversation that engaged his attention. He was eager to learn whether there would be any chance for him to conduct in California but with Italian diplomacy he did not openly speak his thoughts. Rather he talked about the influence that music exerted in Italy. Concerts are a matter of interest to Mussolini and the orchestra of the Augusteo is subsidized by the government. Through Mussolini's patronage the Augusteo Orchestra has been strengthened into a symphonic ensemble which is the pride of Rome.

"What is Mussolini doing now?" asked one of the guests.

"Building his wonderful city for the working people, just outside of Rome and extending Italy's roadways."

"How," Molinari was asked, "can Mussolini finance all these projects?"

"Because," he replied, "Mussolini is prepared for everything that he does. He finances his projects with government money and is always ready to meet all his debts."

"They call Mussolini the modern Napoleon," continued Molinari while his thoughtful eyes traveled to include each one of us in his earnest gaze, "but Mussolini is not like Napoleon, who sought honors for himself and his own family, to whom he gave offices. Mussolini does not exalt himself, his wife, or his children; only the State counts."

Changing from Italian to French, Molinari half whispered:

"*Un homme très fort, très serieux, avec un grand coeur.*"

"Does Mussolini continue to study and improve himself?" asked the interested guest.

"Always," replied Molinari. "He stops at nothing. Nothing is too small for him in the interests of the State. At one time while traveling, Mussolini was given police protection but refused it. An anti-Fascist approached him and the suspicious guards were about to drive him away. Mussolini protested and drew the man into conversation. At the close of the interview he wrote down the man's name and address. From Rome he sent the Fascist literature to his acquaintance, who became a convert."

"What of your other great Italian, Toscanini?" asked Molinari's companion.

"What a genius!" answered Molinari reverently. "He is complete. Some leaders have force and no taste; some have taste and no style; but Toscanini has everything."

"Was there ever another conductor as great as Toscanini, *Maestro?*" inquired Philip Murray.

"I don't believe so; perhaps Nikisch," answered Molinari. "He more nearly approached Toscanini than any other leader."

"Jeritza is singing in *Turandot* this afternoon and I have a box. Shall we go down to the Metropolitan?" suggested Murray.

"Oh! that's the new Puccini work, isn't it?" Margherita asked as she enveloped herself in the fur coat which had just been captured with a pile of winter wraps from the neat little maid at the entrance to the coat-room.

"Yes. You will all enjoy seeing the gorgeous costumes that Jeritza is wearing," explained Murray through teeth that were closed upon a fresh cigarette which he was lighting from the spurting, blue flame of a cleverly designed Russian cigarette lighter.

The shrill January winds cut like cold steel scythes about us as we stepped into the streets to look for our motor. Avenues were jammed with traffic and teeming with men and women who were

driving weary bodies against the small hurricane
that constantly pressed backward the bits of struggling humanity. Blurred forms buttoned under
thick overcoats, with heads lowered into deep coat
collars, sought shelter from the fronts of tall buildings; and the grey or brown soft hats, pulled far
down over foreheads, gave a sinister cast to the ac-
tions of the storm-driven crowd. We drove through
Fifty-ninth Street, passing Central Park, from
whose great arterial roadway streamed hundreds
of beautiful cars. Al Jolson's Theatre, blazing with
lights, had a long file of people pushing towards
the box office.

"What an escape amusement is," I marveled.
"Here are all these people going to absurdly expensive entertainment hoping thereby to refresh
their tired minds."

At last the Metropolitan. The curtain was up
and Tokatyan as the Prince, was singing to a vision
appearing before him in a sheen of light that broke
the darkness on the stage like the radiance of a
star. Dazzled by the illumination we groped our
way into Gatti-Casazza's box.

IX

A TOSCANINI TRIUMPH

A PROCESSION of men and ideas marched and counter-marched through my mind in a continuous pageant as, with the help of Arthur Judson, I studied the schedules which displayed the names of world famous artists.

We were preparing a parade which should take in Los Angeles, San Francisco, and Hillsborough, and, as we hoped for packed grandstands or auditoriums, we made our decisions slowly and thoughtfully.

At last all was in readiness, and Coates, Molinari, and Gabrilowitsch were the directors chosen to lead music through the summer events in Hillsborough and San Francisco.

With Woodland Theatre now able to obtain all the advantages that would accrue through alliance with our big and powerful associates I was ready to leave for home feeling that we had commenced our new plans aided by all that foresight could offer towards our ultimate success.

In the days before departure New York's myriad fascinations cast their spell upon me. The towers of colored marble and granite, the dazzling polished avenues, the shrill police whistles, the arrogant hotel porters, the vigilant eyes of pedestrians, the click of their quickly marching feet excited in me a thrill that quickened before the city's pompous splendor.

Occasionally a pair of aristocratic, proud, high-stepping horses, with jingling bits, and nostrils slightly flecked with foam, recreated once again the old street scenes when people who went excursioning had to set off early in the day to cover distances which are now traversed in a brief hour or so by automobile.

Toscanini had returned and the musical interest centered about the first concert he was to give with the New York Philharmonic. Unless one had a friend among the subscribers it was hopeless to try and procure a place for the great Italian's *première* of the season. Margherita de Vecchi asked me to sit in her box to hear the concert and I lingered on in New York for this—the cream of the season's feast for symphony lovers.

A day or so before Toscanini's performance, guided by Margherita's capable hand, I paid a visit to the super-Conductor. A rendezvous with Margherita found me at the Astor Hotel, in which Toscanini occupies an apartment through the weeks of his season in New York. The power of the man I was to see was upon me. All that I had heard and imagined of the aloof, brilliant, earnest, indefatigable Toscanini surged into me, exalting my mood and lifting me to levels of emotion seldom reached in just a mere, contemplated visit to a great personage. Margherita and I slipped through the high-ceilinged corridors of the big hotel and on towards the door of the Toscanini suite. Before I was fully conscious of what was happening the introduction to the *Maestro* was completed and my hand rested in his. I heard him saying:

"So you came from California and Margherita tells me that you have stayed over to hear my concert."

The charm, dignity, and kindliness of Toscanini enveloped me and I hoped that my pounding heart would grow quiet as I did not want to miss anything that happened throughout my interview.

The Toscanini family clustered about us; the two daughters very handsome and alert, and Madame Toscanini, who held in her arms a tiny dog that was the pet of his fond master. Our conversation was of the music in California; of the great audiences at the Hollywood Bowl; and of the poetic beauty of Woodland Theatre.

"When are you coming to conduct for us?" I begged.

The great brown eyes frowned a little.

"It is so far away," he said. "Too far."

"But you wouldn't feel that distance once you had made the trip and given the thousands of people living in the West a chance to hear you! I know that their appreciation would make you forget the long journey."

Toscanini smiled and then spoke with some sadness:

"I don't feel well and I cannot travel."

"He does not like new plans," said one of his daughters to me; "and this winter he has not been in good health, so it distresses him to think of making a long trip to a strange place."

"Yes, I feel too much; and life is so painful; always something comes to make sorrow and unhappiness."

The lines about the mouth of my host deepened and he fell into a reverie, his face half hidden as it rested in his hand.

Grischa Goluboff, a little eight-year-old violin-

Arturo Toscanini

ist, had spoken almost these same words only a few weeks ago in San Francisco when someone dropped a porcelain cup as we were having tea. With clasped hands the boy gazed at the bits of broken china and from his compassionate heart he sighed as he whispered:

"It was so pretty; always something like that happens to make people feel badly."

What could I speak of that would interest Toscanini? Many images whirled about, like sputtering fireworks, in my brain while my lips were dumb. At last a spacious, white building obtruded itself as a subject for conversation and I began to talk of San Francisco's new War Memorial Opera House. For a quarter of an hour Toscanini was entertained by description of the world's most perfectly equipped stage for opera. We discussed the ideal number of seats that should be installed; also the interior design especially constructed for securing perfect visibility. The acoustics, I told Toscanini, were supervised by Clifford Swan and were said to be flawless.

As I rose to say good-bye, Toscanini smiled enchantingly and said:

"Perhaps when that new opera house is finished I will come out and conduct in San Francisco."

Turning to Margherita, Toscanini said:

"I will go to the elevator with you"; then he tucked my arm through his and held my hand as we walked away from his apartment.

All of the cautiousness which I had tried to maintain through my visit, in the fear that I might tire or annoy the indisposed genius, disappeared and I felt that I had been given the friendship of the man who walked at my side.

When next I saw Toscanini he was walking briskly across the stage of Carnegie Hall as the immence audience, filling the auditorium, rose to greet him in a standing salute. The program commenced at once and the house quieted after its noisy cheers and bravos. My neighbor in Margherita's box was beautiful-voiced, smiling Martinelli. It was my first introduction to him but he knew San Francisco so well that we did not linger in the stiffness that so often seizes two strange persons who find themselves forced to sit side by side for an hour or so.

"I am glad he is playing the Brahms C major," I whispered. Martinelli looked at me thoughtfully for a moment, then answered:

"Yes, the major is bright and happy but the

minor key is best for singers; it offers the loveliest medium for the voice."

Our box grew more crowded as the evening advanced. Toscanini's young daughters stood for a little while at the entrance and chattered with us during the intermission.

The occasion, marking as it did, Toscanini's return after his illness, upset the ravens who had croaked that in all probability the *Maestro* had given his last performance with the New York Philharmonic. More power and authority than he had ever shown; more beauty in his greatest achievement—the production of perfect tone—sent the people mad with excitement and enthusiasm. Toscanini's staunch friends and admirers stood or sat proudly watching the applauding crowd.

"Isn't it just as we told you it would be?" questioned their bright victorious glances.

It was indeed a triumphant vindication of the repeated assertion of his supporters—that *there is but one Toscanini*.

Crowded about the famous figure who later received us in the green room, holding the collar of his coat tightly about his overheated body, were many artists—Madame Alda, Felix Salmond, Joseph Lhevinne, Rudolph Ganz and scores of others who stood about chatting. For each one the slim, erect Toscanini had a warm smile and a special message which flashed swiftly from the brown eyes that astonish one with their clear, steady flame of intelligence while in the same moment they reassure the timid by their candor and tenderness.

X

TEA WITH ALEXANDER SMALLENS

"Drive to the East River, over Fifty-seventh Street," directed Olin Downes.

Marion Browne, Olin, and I were on our way for a cup of tea with Alexander Smallens. We had spent the afternoon at the Metropolitan where Bodansky had conducted a requiem mass in tribute to the memory of that staunch and able friend of music, Harriet Lanier. Smallens drifting into our box for a few moments asked us to visit him on our way uptown. As Olin demurred—protesting that he would be late in getting home and that there was still an evening concert to be reviewed—Marion, with disappointment in her voice, urged her husband to change his mind:

"It will be lovely on the river at this time of day, Olin," she pleaded.

Marion won her point and we timed our trip back to the Downes' apartment to provide the half-hour for tea with Smallens.

Past gay, flower-filled balconies—avoiding excited children still playing in the streets at this late hour—we rushed with the traffic towards that portion of the bank of the East River directly opposite the penitentiary and the other buildings that dot Welfare Island. Lights from the vessels silently gliding from the dark water, blinked in salutation to the great city and shone upon the stone walls that were having their daily drenching by the little ripples of the evening tide.

Olin chatted on. Turning to me he said:

"Smallens is to have a concert with your Philharmonic, isn't he?"

"Yes," I replied; "perhaps not this year but surely in some future season."

"I am glad to hear that," Olin commented, "for Smallens is a sound musician and in every respect so honest and sincere. You know, of course, that he was entirely an operatic leader until recently, when he accepted a post with the Philadelphia Orchestra."

"Don't you think that Alexander looks exactly like the King of Spain?" asked Marion. "I can see the same long face and deep-set dark eyes that make Alphonso's expression so distinctive."

"Yes, he has the Bourbon features and he might

very easily be taken for the twin brother of the King. Smallens says that often he is stared at by people who pass him in the street and are sure that they have rubbed elbows with a near relative of Spain's ex-King; but Smallens has lived always in New York and was educated here. I think," continued Olin, "that some of his finest conducting was done for Pavlova and there is no question that she danced most gloriously when Smallens was leading the orchestra. He could always manage her even in the most difficult of her moods and he seemed to possess some superlative authority that she respected."

The motor stopped before the door of a high building and we stepped from the front entrance into the elevator which carried us up to the Smallens suite. The vestibule door was standing open, in friendly fashion, and about the tea table in the library were already seated a number of Alexander's friends. Our host greeted us with both hands stretched before him in a lovely gesture of welcome. Grasping one of Marion's hands and one of mine—at the same time—he led us into the room and over to a couch where we saw a middle-aged, foreign-looking little woman glancing shyly at us from out of her nook of big, silk pillows.

"This is my mother," Smallens explained. The steady eyes of the Polish woman looked first at Marion, afterward at me, and then she smiled with the same grave but kindly smile that often lighted the dark olive face of her son. She next patted the cushions and said:

"There is plenty of room for us all in this big seat."

Marion and I dropped on to the couch while Olin took a little chair which did not look as if it could long withstand the strain of holding up his big, sturdy form.

Smallens bustled about with the tea things.

"What stunning jade green china!" exclaimed Marion as a fragile little cup was placed in her hand.

"Do you like it? You will never guess where I bought it," said Alexander.

"Tell me, will you? But then I suppose it is useless even to want to know, for I could not buy any china just now."

"Neither could I," agreed Smallens, "but I annexed these at the five-and-ten cent store together with all of the stuff that you see about here."

"You have a great eye for color, Alexander," Olin continued dwelling on the theme of the jade

cups. "Now I never would think of choosing anything so pleasing as these."

"See, this is where I keep everything," interrupted Smallens. And as his fingers pressed a little
smooth panel in the wall the wooden frame opened
and we could see tiers of dishes, and pots of jam,
and jars of olives, standing in neat rows ready for
the parties that were so delightful a part of the conductor's social life.

"Now I will show you my real treasure." As
Smallens spoke he moved towards the bedroom
door:

"What is it?" asked Marion.

"*My* Olin," answered Smallens. "I don't mean
your Olin, Marion, but mine."

"What in heaven's name are you talking about!"
protested Marion.

"A lovely big carved image of Buddha that I
bought when I was in San Francisco," explained
Smallens. "I call him 'Olin' because he has such
a happy, comfortable look about him. The man
that sold me the figure said that it was very old and
you can see worm holes in the wood; but then, of
course, that does not necessarily mean age. Such
clever fakes are made these days that it takes an
expert to be sure of the genuine thing."

"Who took you to the shop where you bought the Buddha?" asked Marion.

"No one; I just dropped into a Chinese store one day as I was rambling through San Francisco streets. I had seen the image in the window of this place on one of my walks and had determined to have it if the price wasn't too steep. 'How much do you want for it?' I asked the Chinese shop-keeper.

" 'Fifty dollars,' he replied.

"Of course I know that it is never wise to jump at the first price quoted by one of these curio deal-ers but I listened to all the man's talk about the image being worth a great deal more and of how it had been smuggled out of a Tibetan temple, so I gave the old fellow what he asked for the an-tique."

"Maybe you can tell me what it is worth," said Smallens turning to me, "for you must see a lot of Oriental curios in California."

"I do see many of them," I answered with feel-ing as I remembered the cheap porcelains and gaudy silks that hang in the show cases of China-town—displayed together with little paper fans and tiny ivory elephants for the souvenir seekers.

"Wait a minute, I will get my Buddha," said

Smallens as he stepped into the next room. In a moment he reappeared with the fat, unctuous-looking idol, which he placed on the broad sill of the window that overlooked the East River.

Dusk filtered into the little library from the immense pools of darkness that encircle the great apartment houses of New York. The silence that had touched the mood of her guests as they watched the slowly falling night was broken by Mrs. Smallens:

"Alexander," she said in a low voice, "I brought you something today that I found among some of your things."

"What is it, Mother?" asked Smallens.

"Here it is. Look!"

Smallens stretched out a hand towards a kodak picture which his mother placed in his hand.

"Pavlova!" he murmured. "Yes, I remember well this was taken in the garden at Cannes. How gay she was that day! See, Olin, isn't it a good likeness?"

Smallens was far away from us as he stood with bent head looking dreamily at the little photograph. Then abruptly he changed the subject:

"Who is going to the all-Wagner program of Toscanini to-night?"

"We are *all* going," replied Olin quickly, "which means that we have to leave here this minute."

Briskly we made our way to the street with Smallens calling after us:

"See you later; don't be late. Toscanini will do that program magnificently."

XI

ALL ABOARD

IT WAS my final day in New York. Surrounded by trunks and suitcases I sat waiting for the masterful hands of a porter while I snatched a sandwich. A few friends who were scattered about the tiny sitting room at the hotel rained final advice upon topics which we had been discussing for days.

"Remember that Coates does Scriabin better than anyone else and be sure and have him give you Vaughan Williams' *London Symphony*," put in Harold Balton.

"Molinari has a good arrangement of Debussy's *L'Isle Joyeuse* which he has transcribed; get him to play it for you," suggested Olin Downes.

"Here's the porter," shouted someone above the din of voices.

With seven persons jammed in the motor we pressed through the thick sluggish traffic of the city.

"You are just going to make it," concluded Marion Downes, who had been looking at her wrist-watch.

71

I was exasperated. "Why have I not allowed my-self more time?" I asked myself irritably as I dug my toes into the floor-board of the motor. The tower of the Grand Central burst into view just as I had planned to ring up some of my friends from the station telling them that I had missed the train.

"Don't let us lose touch with you," called out Olin as the long Twentieth Century pulled slowly out from the heavy concrete tunnels.

I took my place by the window in the little drawing room and pressed close to the glass for a last survey of the streets of New York. Under me the wheels of the big steel car turned smoothly in so many revolutions to the minute that I could not imagine how we could glide along so noise-lessly, so easily. The bright flowers, the baskets of fruit, the gaily painted covers of magazines, and the pungent strands of cigarette smoke all filled the little drawing room with the dear vibrant im-ages of the givers of the gifts. Life, I reflected for the twenty millionth time, is wonderful.

At Chicago I was to meet the new president of the Philharmonic. During that wash-up hour or two that we have before our Overland Limited pulls out for San Francisco I rushed to the Blackstone Hotel and there I found Charles Blyth waiting for me. We went over all that had happened since the time of sending in my letter of resignation to the Board.

Charlie's steady, business-like tones pinned my attention when it flagged—overwhelmed by the attraction of the sounds in the street below. Night was falling; the pavements were beginning to shine under the artificial lights; jets from the crowd—hurrying past the tall office buildings—darted jerkily across at street corners. I was spellbound and had to tear myself away from the throngs surging out there in the dusk.

"As I just said," spoke Charlie very decidedly, "if you have got the show there is nothing to it."

I felt suddenly very tired, very incapable, and very lonely.

"Oh, never mind, Charlie; we can't plan everything too far ahead," I protested wearily.

"Well, I am glad you feel all right about it at any rate," he said.

"Certainly I do," I replied quickly and emphatically.

"All right. Good-bye; I'll see you in California."

Charlie was off for New York.

With my bags, heavy fur coat, and books I, too,

was off for the long stretch of level prairie land that led to the mountains and from the mountains to the sea.

The little towns we see along the cross-continent route always pique me into speculation about their characters. My curiosity reaches its climax when the train pulls pompously and importantly to a standstill before the small, dismal stations that serve as ports for travellers. Mystifying persons—all done up in great coats and soggy, thick, felt caps and carrying swinging lanterns—come with apologetic authority over to the train where they begin to thump the wheels and car couplings; or peer under the coaches with flame torches. Disgorged passengers crunch over the graveled roadbed to inspect the fruit stands and to hail the spruce young telegraph boy who threads his way through the slush as he waves his yellow envelopes. Standing at attention beside their little Brussels-carpeted steps are the white-jacketed porters; with arms folded across their important chests they keep watch over their flocks lest they stray dangerously far from the Pullmans.

"All aboard," floats the command; and high-heeled ladies grasp the arms of their escorts as they rush breathlessly to seize the cold metal supports of the vestibule railings. Once more the "iron horse" snorts and plunges into the spikes of light that glint along the rails and dapple the swaying cars with tiny gold discs falling earthward from the descending sun.

XII

ARTHUR POPE EQUIPS THE THEATRE

How quickly the excitement of an undertaking dies when the promoter discovers that the majority of those who should be most deeply concerned are wholly indifferent, or even antagonistic, to the project. It gives the same impression as when one makes a trip to a tropical country prepared for a hot climate, outfitted with bathing suits and cool seaside costumes, only to find that the weather of the country has changed and that the people have gone in for wools and furs.

Such a puzzling situation greeted me when I reached California. The Philharmonic and its bickerings were "ancient history" which no one wanted to hear mentioned. I read a little warning in the attitude of my friends which made me avoid discussing the coming Summer Concerts until the time approached for their inauguration. Turning to the outside world I found sympathy and understanding in the masses that would come to hear our music. The days were dull and disheartening at times. What could be done to make the neighborhood once more curious about Our Theatre?

Arthur Upham Pope had a plan for redecorating the stage. Charles Blyth, our president, had returned from his eastern trip and he had formed his new committees. At a meeting of the executive committee it was decided to follow the Pope suggestion of an entirely new stage setting and to give the equipping of the theatre to Pope, who, because of his intimate acquaintance with Byzantine and Greek architecture, had long cherished a desire to create an out-of-door theatre in the colors and designs used by the ancients.

The Hillsborough School trustees who controlled the rights of the property on which our theatre stood, informed us that—as school would be in session until a week before our first concert took place—we would be prohibited from commencing our construction work and redecoration until the term had ended. This would give us just nine days for the erection of the shell and the placing of a new covering over the exposed section of the theatre. School officers had agreed to put up the shell over the stage for the improvement of the acoustics but the ornamentation was to be our affair.

The current of gossip that so wonderfully enlivens country life began to whisper that the new stage-setting of the theatre would be worth seeing. Arthur Pope soon had his architect, John McCool, and his contractor, Dan Wallace, at work on the new scheme. From the Pope collection of architectural drawings the plans evolved.

It was Arthur's idea to represent the rhythm and color of music by corresponding patterns and hues in the decoration on the walls of the shell. All his imagination and love of music were devoted to the task of symbolizing the forms of music in his designs for the Theatre. Upon the back wall of the stage was a design of gold wheels embossed upon a turquoise background. The figures in this space were so related that they represented the unity of design in the sonata and symphony.

It was also Arthur's idea to have his motifs representative of action such as take place in the ballet. The similarity of form in painting and music is recognized and taught in some schools where paintings are divided for study into one-part, two-part, or three-part song forms. Arthur Pope was interested in making his scenery convey the relationship between the two arts by means of the symbolic and geometrical portrayal of form.

Subscription books began to sell as sightseers

were stimulated by the brilliant effect of our stage. The dreadful nightmare of inaction and torpor which had hung about us was dispelled by the unusual note in the Woodland Theatre arrangements and we felt that when the opening day drew near some sort of a crowd would venture into our enclosure to admire those gaily stenciled awnings with their blue Roman borders.

A crew of workmen at the theatre grounds labored far into the nights to finish the elaborate embossings. We served them with hot coffee, sandwiches, and cigarettes to encourage them to continue painting the difficult rhythmic patterns and numerous themes.

The San Mateo *Times* and the Burlingame *Advance* sent their music critics to inspect the much-discussed structure and the enterprising and generous editors of these newspapers poured out upon their front pages great headlines praising the concerts and the unique style of the fresh decoration. We were classified as one of the leading attractions in California—in the land of outdoor entertainments.

One day at the Burlingame Country Club one of my friends suddenly exploded with curiosity:

"Tell me about the conductors for the summer.

Of course we know all about Gabrilowitsch but
what is this Albert Coates like? And the Italian,
Molinari? Is he good?"

Realizing that I must make every word count,
while I had the attention of my group, I spoke
quickly:

"Coates comes first. I haven't seen him but his
photographs are unusually promising. Perhaps you
know that he is a great friend of Bernard Shaw's
and that Shaw often visits him at his place on the
Italian Lakes." I rambled on: "Shaw is very fond
of music and apparently likes the society of
Coates."

I searched in my handbag and pulled out some
photographs.

"Would you like to see these pictures of Coates,
taken with Bernard Shaw?" I asked.

"He is fascinating, isn't he?" mused a very pretty
woman who was studying the prints I had given
her showing a scene—in the garden of Coates' villa
on Lake Maggiore—snapped in a moment of informal chat between the musician and the Irish
writer. Coates and Shaw sit carelessly in a great
swing, their faces twinkling with merriment over
some jest, most probably a jibe or witticism of
Shaw's. Coates is dressed only in a sport shirt and

very abbreviated shorts. His big muscular legs and arms are bare and his shock of curly brown hair so accentuates the giant stature and strength of the Russian-English conductor that he seems to be some great creature out of a legend.

"Molinari is quite the opposite of Coates in appearance," I explained, "but he has also, unquestionably, great charm and appeal."

"They should be worth hearing," said one of the coterie with decision, and as I saw expectation in the expressions upon the faces of my friends I felt that they had been won over and that I could count upon their support.

My spirits revived as it was easier to undertake the uninteresting duties that were part of the routine in the development of the Philharmonic's future when backed by the encouragement and approval of my friends.

XIII

ALBERT COATES

COATES reached San Francisco a few days before his first concert in Hillsborough on June 24th. My first glimpse of him was at the ferry where his hatless, tousled head, and huge shoulders converted the people about him into a pygmy world. As I walked towards him he cast upon me a captivating smile and in his grey-green eyes was an invitation to friendliness. Colossal in size this great, healthy, buoyant person had something very Irish in his make-up; he seemed to have come from an age of mighty men and as he laughed and talked, like the running water of some swiftly coursing stream, he awakened his listeners and stirred in them waves of unexplainable excitement.

Once in the motor we began to talk programs:

"I want to use Prokofieff's *Love of Three Oranges* at either the first or second concert," Coates urged. "It is interesting and colorful and I have the orchestration with me."

At this moment the grey-green eyes looked humbly into mine while Coates spoke gently:

"Prokofieff is a great friend of mine and I like to place him on my programs whenever I can."

"Let us think it over," I procrastinated, for I had a strange misgiving that too much acquiescence to the requests of my new conductor would lead to his dominating the field.

"Please," continued Coates pleading warmly while he pinned upon me a wheedling stare.

"We will talk it over to-morrow," I suggested.

"Well, if you insist," he answered disappointedly.

To steer my guest into different channels I spoke about the symphony leaders who were to follow him. He knew Molinari and liked his work. Especially he thought him good in eighteenth-century music. And Gabrilowitsch was a splendid musician and a wonderful fellow.

"Have you been much in America?" I asked him.

"Yes, in Rochester where I built up the orchestra and the opera but unfortunately another man is there now getting the cream of my work."

"That's disappointing," I sympathized. "Will you never go back there?"

"Probably not," he jerked out shortly.

"Well, at any rate, there are dozens of interesting places which are clamoring for good orchestra leaders. You will love our little theatre, and of course the Hollywood Bowl is the most thrilling place in the world. And then you will have thousands at your concert in the San Francisco Civic Auditorium."

The expressive eyes and quick smile assured me that I had dispelled the dour recollections of Rochester.

"Where do you live?" Coates asked me abruptly.

"Oh, I have a house in the country. Would you like to come down to-morrow and take luncheon with me? Afterward we can go over to the theatre so that you can get an idea of what your surroundings will be on Sunday."

"What time do I leave San Francisco? I am thinking of rehearsals," explained Coates.

"About noon-time. I will send the car to the Fairmont Hotel and you can drive down to the peninsula, through the park and out by the ocean, where you will have a view from the Skyline Boulevard."

"I would like that," Coates said eagerly, "for I love the sea better than anything in the world except perhaps gardens."

"Then all your loves should be satisfied in California," I replied, "for we have endless miles of water and acres and acres of flowers."

At the portico of the Fairmont Hotel I dropped the guest conductor. Through the swinging doors of the marble entrance-hall I caught sight of familiar figures. The reporters were waiting for their copy.

A strange peace hovered over me on my drive home. Coates, I assured myself, was commanding enough and unusual enough to sway an audience. His striking looks, his persuasive manner, his genuineness would captivate the public and our success was assured.

I floated luxuriously into a half-dream wherein I saw an ideally equipped theatre. Here the acoustics would be right, the light would fall without glare upon the audience, the pitch of the amphitheatre would be at such an angle that each person could see and hear without effort. Just outside the theatre there would be a garden; gay fountains would shower the green leaves of its shaded promenades with bright water-drops. In a little plaza there would be a restaurant filled with mushroom-topped umbrellas and sociable little tables upon which would be placed stone mugs of cold things to drink. About these tables would be seated the people who came from afar every Sunday to listen to our concerts.

Day-dreaming was entertaining but far more to the point were the real signs on the billboards which I passed by the roadside. On these the advertising firm of Foster and Kleiser had generously posted the announcements of our concerts. The yellow sheets blazed forth, in red and black letters, our concert dates and the names of our orchestra leaders. Farther on, banners over the roadways trailed like great stationary kites. All these guides to the theatre, and the community interest in what was taking place were more bracing to my hopes than any other demonstration could have been.

I dropped in at the Theatre to see what progress had been made. Grace Robbins, Helen Chesebrough, and a committee of women, appointed by the Hillsborough Garden Club, were planting the circular flower-beds under the oak trees with purple cineraria and petunias. Edward Schroeder, and his crew of gardeners, had filled the ravine with mountain ferns. Upon the side walls of the stage were the tall cypress spires; so solemn and so still, they framed in the orchestra-setting with their own note of formal design, showing that nature, like music, enjoys the classic style.

Lusty-voiced, big-bodied Albert Coates was seized upon by civic clubs, musical societies, and society hostesses, who exploited him as the honored guest for their breakfasts and luncheons. Where groups were looking for diversion Coates was a magnet. To be sure, excited discussions frequently arose after his departure from drawing-rooms, or reception halls, as in company his volatile nature occasionally exploded into a joke, or some frank exhibition of feeling, which ruffled persons who were unsympathetic to such conduct. Coates dominated his world during the ten days which he spent in San Francisco. His vivid conversation, which often blazed at white heat, when he was hurrying bareheaded with friends through the city's streets puzzled passers-by and aroused an interest reminiscent of another Englishman, made famous in the old ballad of John Gilpin, whose pranks through England's countryside upset the decorum of respectable, God-fearing citizens.

At times our guest artist assumed a dignified gait and deportment and scarcely spoke except to answer with great formality any questions asked of him. When he was in this solemn mood we addressed him as the "Archbishop of Canterbury."

Coates spoke of his tastes and ambitions during long days spent in our garden. Mannerisms were put aside and the problems of the profession were presented to us while his eyes wandered over the sparkling, sunlit valley that opened below our hill.

"My winters are spent in Barcelona," Coates explained rapidly. "Our opera there, which I conduct, is subsidized by the government. We use home-talent for the chorus but we import our leads from the countries in whose language the operas we give are to be sung. For example, if we have *Boris Godunoff* our stars will be acquired from Russia; if we sing *Louise* the artists come from Paris. It makes a splendid ensemble and gives the local people confidence to be headed by singers who are sure of the words. The spirit of the work is better presented when the chief characters can infuse into it the atmosphere which the composer had in mind when he wrote his score."

Scholars Cottage, home of the Pope Ackermans, was turned over to Coates and there for so many hours a day he worked on his opera *Samuel Pepys*. Early suppers at the cottage were whetted by philosophical discussions, Arthur and Phyllis entertaining their guest by analyzing problems which his inquiring mind brought up for investigation. Old theories and platitudes were left slaughtered in cold-blood struck by the keen-edged logic of the two philosophers.

Coates watching, with admiration in his sharp eyes, would finally tear himself away from the table and hurl himself at the big Steinway. Here he was the master as through the dark polished wood of the room the Coates scherzo and *Minuette d'Amour* set the glistening pewter cups swinging against the blackened panels. The huge frame at the piano, clad in loose tweeds and sport shirt, opening away from a strong brown throat, was flung into a vortex of sound in which swift, sure hands formed smashing chords and staccato figures. Coates was storming heaven to bring back the lightning and the thunder roving there among the caverns and crags. A little clock standing on the mantelpiece, between two stone Persian horses with martial tails and manes, ticked on in un-broken regularity, its mechanical beating out of the time acting as an uncompromising pace-maker against the syncopated rhythm of the scherzo. By the fireside a tortoise-shell cat crooned her hearth-song and at times Coates turned his head away from the music as the snap of eucalyptus logs quickened the air, perfuming it with a stinging balsam. In these surroundings *Samuel Pepys* thrived, and his gossipings and meanderings trailed and spread in widening arcs of octaves and chromatic runs. The occupants of the room grew small and insignificant; nothing seemed to exist except Pepys' pattering footsteps and the wag of his clacking tongue.

The curiosity of concert addicts grew tense and alive during the last few days of publicizing before our first performance. Coates' candor, Arthur's decorations, and the public's general willingness to have a part in our entertainment bade fair to offer something of merit and of piquant interest.

Our vice-president, loyal and energetic Grace Robbins, telephoned me the day before our season opened to ask if we were assured of a large crowd; if not she wanted to buy up all the unsold seats, which would be distributed about the neighborhood. She emphatically declared, "That theatre has to be jammed to-morrow."

"You won't have to buy those seats," I answered through the brine of a few grateful tears, "but God bless you for your support."

Heavy night winds always do a great deal of damage to the floating covering of our amphitheatre. In the early morning hours of our opening day I woke at intervals to listen to the rustle of the trees by which I could gauge the amount of wind that we might have to face. The air seemed quiet but I said to myself, "Perhaps it only appears to be still because I want it to be so." Anxiously I argued further, "Maybe there is a wind over at the theatre that is tearing our awning to bits." From my window I saw the morning break. The heavens were flecked with white but a shimmer over this "fisherman's sky" foretold hot weather. My hopes were high, for this kind of a day would bring people to the country.

Three o'clock, the concert hour, approached. The theatre filled rapidly. Within the boxes, roped off with orange-colored cords, were seated the patrons of the Philharmonic. Through the subscription-book sections also were scattered sponsors and committee members. The amphitheatre had the look of a large, richly inlaid chess-board upon which kings, queens, knights, and pawns were posed.

"This is a great day, isn't it?" called out our staunch patron William H. Crocker as he passed my box. "Look at that line! It reaches to the entrance gate and they are still coming in."

Coates at this moment walked out upon the stage and the audience became electrified. He acknowledged the applause, then he spoke to the crowd, explaining to them that the shell upon the stage was new and as a means of testing the acoustics he would play a few measures of the *Oberon* Overture. Then he would stop the orchestra for a few seconds after which he would repeat the Overture in its entirety. This little bit of showmanship amused the audience, who followed the acting of Coates with expectation until the *Oberon* tinkled out in fairy-like tones. The acoustics played no tricks and soon the program was under way.

Vaughan Williams' *London Symphony* was the large work played by Coates. It is one of the most interesting compositions by a present-day contributor to symphonic literature. In the foggy, muffled music London seemed spread before us. The calm, sweeping waters of the Thames flow silently beneath the mist-chilled dawn. Westminster chimes are heard striking the half-hour. Suddenly we are in the Strand where newsboys are shouting, and buses and taxis are hurrying noisily by in the early morning traffic. The grating voices of the shouting costers speak characteristically of London. A concertina plays a dance-tune. Its gay measures sent my thoughts to London streets. I remembered, in a glow of happy recollections, my last drive through the grey-shrouded pavements. The air was perfumed with violets and the dull tramp of unseen people, walking on the sidewalks, moved me by the ghostly quality of their march through the gloom.

At the intermission Yehudi Menuhin and Mischa Elman visited our box. Yehudi's handsome thoughtful face warmed into a radiant smile when asked what he thought of music in the open air.

"I like it!" he exclaimed. "It makes you listen in order to get the music through the out-of-door sounds. It is great!"

Elman praised Piastro's powerful tone:

"Really," he said, "he is a great artist. When I say that I enjoy hearing him so much it should mean a great deal; for it is said that an artist only enjoys hearing himself play." Elman spoke with humor but there was seriousness in his tribute.

Elman, Yehudi, and I strolled to the orangeade stand in the playground. A large portion of the audience were moving about in the spacious promenade court. Adeline Fuller, the able chairman of our box committee, was standing by the refreshment booth talking to Helen Cameron, Ethel

Henderson, Mortimer Fleishacker, and Milton Esberg. They were discussing a new plan for rearranging the seats in the theatre. Ruth Tobin, William Leib, Edith Chamberlain, and Elsa Wiel, members of our executive board, were grouped near the big oak as they reviewed the concert. Celia Clark strolled out through an exit to show her guests—Mrs. Elizabeth Sprague Coolidge and the members of the Pro Arte Quartet—our outdoor planting. Agnes Clark and Gunnar Johansen crossed the courtyard to speak to Elman and Yehudi. Agnes and Gunnar had both appeared as soloists with the Philharmonic in piano concertos. Towards the grove of poplars by the side wall was congregated our woman's committee. Representative of the county's best interests, in their number are librarians, music teachers, reporters—all women of importance in the business and professional ranks of the vicinity.

Suddenly the trumpets announced that the intermission was over. People swarmed back to the theatre for the final numbers and to storm Coates —who was recalled again and again—with bravos and applause. About my box were the smiling faces of the hosts of friends which the Philharmonic had gathered in its short history. I felt the hum of a satisfied public and I listened with content, for it indicated that our endeavor to rescue the Philharmonic from failure and extinction had ended in success.

XIV

SAN FRANCISCO WELCOMES
BERNARDINO MOLINARI

WHEN Molinari, the little leader from Rome, and his pretty wife Mary arrived, the roof of the ferry building echoed exultantly to the gay, excited voices and the voluble speech of the Italian compatriots who came in splendid array to greet their countryman. The *Maestro* looked exactly as he had on the winter's day in New York when he had discussed the possibility of his coming to California. His grey, soft hat was perched at the perky angle which I well remembered, but I missed the dashing green overcoat with the grey astrachan collar, for now it was summer. Bright were the dimpled smiles of Madame Molinari as she accepted the flowers offered her by Madame Silva and listened to the fervid, welcoming words of the committee. The whole party was soon off in motors to the Fairmont Hotel. Ahead of the speeding cars was an escort of motorcycle police whose sirens sent the citizens scurrying before their screaming blasts.

Molinari was in a conflict of emotions, for he was flushed with the excitement and pleasure of his warm greeting but was sad, melancholy, and frowning as he said to me:

"I understand that they are not going to permit me to play Respighi's *The Pines of Rome.*"

"I know, *Maestro,*" I confessed. "It was decided not to give this number on account of the heavy royalty and the extra instruments needed in the orchestra."

"But if I am just to give compositions that any-one can play, and not to have a chance to show what I am able to do, why do they ask me to come here?" he pleaded.

I yielded to the misery in his eyes:

"Wait until I talk it over again with Joseph Thompson, the president of the San Francisco Summer Symphony," I suggested. "Perhaps, after all, some way can be found for you to give *The Pines.*"

"Do please, Madame," he half whispered and, as I turned towards the earnest, unhappy, mobile face which looked sorrowfully out over the terra-cotta hills that circled the city, I decided that we would play that Italian number if we had to raise a special public purse to pay for it.

I am sure Molinari felt my sympathy and interest, for he brightened as we neared the big hotel on the top of the California Street hill. In his intelligent eyes there was a steady look as if he were assured that his request had already been granted so that he felt free to include in his program the Respighi number which was the work he had traveled from Rome especially to conduct.

In the Civic Auditorium of San Francisco the next day I tiptoed down the aisle just as Molinari bowed to the orchestra and raised his stick. He stood poised with his left hand gracefully resting upon the curve of his waistline. It was his first rehearsal and I wondered what number he would play. With true dignity and great purpose in his voice he announced: *"Pini di Roma."* From a seat near by in the dim auditorium I caught a fleeting look from Joe Thompson. The expression on Joe's face was humble and quiet and I knew that the man from Rome had won his first victory over us.

Alfred Metzger, the chairman of the music committee of the San Francisco Summer Symphony, who was sitting next to me, smiled tolerantly; then said:

"Molinari was determined he would get Respighi on the program. What could we do?"

Bernardino Molinari

"Nothing," I replied. "Really nothing!"

A new regime for the orchestra was inaugurated and soon put into action by the determined and Spartan spirit of Molinari. His insistence upon exactness, his attention to detail and to the intention which the composer had in mind when making his score created an atmosphere of discipline which had not before surrounded our orchestra in so superlative a degree. To steal with greatest caution into the big hall during rehearsal is to know the courageous, painstaking attitude that Molinari brings to each and every number on his programs.

XV

A CLOSE-UP OF MOLINARI

DOWN the aisles of the auditorium floats his fervid voice:

"La, la, la, l——a." It is rehearsal time and Molinari is singing with the orchestra. "Te te; ta ta;—*fortissimo*—la, le, la,—*con espressione,*" calls out the earnest little leader.

The men bend to their instruments in the *Tannhäuser* Overture while exaltation and excitement play over their intent faces. The short, strong, graceful body of Molinari sways upon the tiny platform. He turns to the left fluttering his fingers towards the first violins whose bows drop into position then sweep across the arched sounding boards.

"*Pianissimo,*" warns Molinari with the forefinger of his right hand touching his lips in eloquent illustration. From the far corner, almost hidden by tiers of 'cellos, woodwinds, and brasses, the drums begin to peal. Molinari sings on more fervently and his baton delicately traces triangles and squares upon space as he counts. His ear listens for imperfections but the music is flawlessly played.

"Bene," whispers the director.

This is the hour when the *Maestro* cajoles, scolds, coaxes the personnel of the orchestra into accepting his interpretations. The players must be entirely dominated by the ideas of the leader. To the uninitiated it is often hard to know just why the orchestra is quickly checked in some fine phrase by the sharp and authoritative rap of the baton upon the desk. A lovely languid song is flowing gently upon the soul when the lordly rat-tat-tat strikes irritably upon our abstracted mood. The music rushes madly forward unable to lose the momentum it has gained and dies in meaningless figures. Listeners stifle a sigh of exasperation, and the dozens of pairs of eyes, which had been fixed upon the scores, move upward and rove from the racks and their white sheets to gaze at Molinari. Piastro the concert-master is not relaxing his attention, however, but leaning from his chair he discusses with Molinari the phrase which has not suited the alert leader.

"Not so . . . but—so," explaining Molinari, sawing across his arm with his stick to indicate the bowing he wants to have used.

Piastro shows the score marked with the old

phrasing as an excuse for the mistake. Molinari
makes a grimace and shrugs his shoulders plainly
saying:

"Well, whoever made that idiotic bit of expression, better were it that he should never have been
born, or having been born that he should be left
to die uncared for."

Piastro and his teammate, Fenster, scrub out the
old pencil marks and write in the new *tempi*. After
their scribbling has been communicated to the orchestra, rat-tat-tat goes the baton and we are off
again on the pyramiding blocks of sound.

Again Molinari sings:

The tambourines clink like the gold bangles on
the anklets of dancing girls. The heated air of the
artificially lighted rehearsal hall contrasts cheaply
with the beauty of a summer's day glimpsed
through a streaked skylight. Nobly the music
dashes its splendor to heaven and to the four quarters of the earth. The orchestra is now treading
along a highway which is fragrant with immortal
flowers. The little company of listeners become
part of the rich harmonies about them and like a
band of awakened spirits they soar with the orchestra battalion as it mounts upward in a succes-
sion of triumphant charges.

Solemnly the big clock above the balcony points to eleven. Molinari's arms fall to his side. He shuts his score and the players release their instruments from the clutch of tired hands. The audience rises from the hard, wooden chairs still half dazed. All begin donning coats, scarfs, and hats. Some strange shrinking process seems to be going on within us as the spell of the music lifts. Once again we are all just humble living things with human interests and we drop into our rôles of fathers, brothers, kinsmen, friends.

Not always do things go so smoothly at a Molinari rehearsal. There are days when the soft brown eyes of Mary Molinari dwell persistently upon the purse, or the fur neckpiece resting in her lap. She is sitting helplessly by while her Bernardino indulges in a gust of temperament. In torrential outbursts the Molinari nature, obsessed by the urge for perfection, plays whirlwind havoc with the orchestra as his strong, tense body shakes with exasperation over misunderstood orders or bungled interpretations. Everyone within earshot is thrown into a panic and all are drawing suffocated breaths as they hear the storm descending. What will Molinari do next? Eyes furtively glance towards the nearest neighbor and they ask unspoken questions. How long will the fury remain unleashed? Will the orchestra take it on the chin? Will they rise and walk out? Or will Molinari leave? It doesn't seem as if the men could endure much longer. Something must happen to end the black terror which is spreading. The scourging continues. The white face of Molinari is "weeping." From his closed teeth come sharp crisp corrections that drop with precision like well-aimed and swiftly hurled steel knives.

Molinari begins to look exhausted like an overwrought actor. The orchestra seems spiritless and frustrated. The whole action of the scene is pinned upon the movements of the conductor. His expression settles into boyish innocence.

"Fini," he commands.

The subdued voice of Mary Molinari is heard to whisper:

"Grâce à Dieu!"

We creep from the hall in a bewildered fashion, glad to escape without having the house pulled down upon our heads. Glancing back the vigorous Italian director is seen surrounded by his men. He is telling anecdotes in a clear voice from which all trace of emotion has gone.

"What a technician! An amazing person is he

not, Madame?" remarks a big fellow who is shuf-
fling by me with a 'cello under his arm.

I regarded this simple being with respect. He
had completely forgotten the last painful two
hours.

"Amazing!" I agreed quietly.

Molinari's first concert was blessed by serene
skies. Crowds filled the tiers of seats to the outer
boundaries of the theatre. Many of our patrons had
heard, through those secret channels of rumor, that
the orchestra had gone through a siege of drilling
and they wanted to behold the results.

Molinari stepped through the door opening
upon the flight of stone stairs that descend to the
stage. His erect, buoyant figure stood poised for a
moment upon the first step as his eyes looked into
the distance, beyond the audience, then traveled
back over the sea of faces which were composed
and upturned to his as with decisiveness he walked
lightly down to the podium. Another moment or
two passed while the orchestra settled themselves
to be in readiness for the opening signal. They
could be seen reading Molinari's thoughts: At last
in perfect unison with the first up-beat of his stick,
a wave of sound quivered into the sunshine. A gust
of falling wind shifted the music so that it dwindled

in volume but in a second the tone of the orchestra became steady and strong as outward-bound the harmonies filled the air.

Under the red glow of the painted awning people stirred rapturously. There were numbers on the program which were fresh and interesting— Debussy's *L'Isle Joyeuse,* transcribed by Molinari, the enchanting Corelli suite for strings, Respighi's *The Pines of Rome.* The crowd swayed and shouted in the Respighi when the Roman consul's army marches at dawn over the Appian Way. In a slow, monotonous rhythm the thundering legions of cavalry sweep to the blare of trumpets over the road that leads to the Eternal City.

In one section of *The Pines of Rome* a phonograph record is played upon which has been recorded the song of the nightingale. Birds that fluttered in and out among the boughs of the oaks which shade our theatre began to sing as they heard the trilling of the nightingale. Their melody at first was timid and low but finally carried away by the sheer ecstasy of singing they silenced the music on the stage, continuing their chorus until the horns' deep-toned sonorities frightened them into silence.

XVI

NOEL SULLIVAN'S HOUSE

MOLINARI still clutched his brown leather port-
folio containing the precious scores that he had
just played in Woodland Theatre.

"Comme cette Haydn est belle," commented
Molinari softly.

"Oui et que vous avez mastered it," agreed Olin
Downes in tones of fervent praise.

Molinari laughing at Olin's broken French gaily
expanded into details.

"I studied it with Nikisch."

"It takes an Italian to do it as it should be done,"
Olin interrupted. "It is, like the Italian manner,
courtly and suave and light. How do you manage
it so perfectly, *Maestro?"*

Molinari's grey eyes grew sober and there crept
into them something of the remoteness of a soul
which has effaced itself in laboring for a required
degree of perfection that only immolation and determination can secure.

"I study the score sometimes for six or seven

months before I transmit it to the orchestra,"
Molinari said quietly. "One must have it thor-
oughly impressed upon, and arranged in, his own
mind before he directs it. In this way all the fine
material is kept."

"Did you notice," Molinari asked eagerly, "how
much like Rossini Haydn is?"

"Yes, the same pretty devices serve them both,"
remarked Olin.

"But to go on to the Germans," he continued. "I
was surprised to find myself succumbing once again
to the *Lohengrin*. It's great stuff. One can hear in
the prelude the origin of so much of our modern
music. Sometimes I think I never want to hear another note of Wagner and then I listen again and
I realize what unmatched material much of it is.
I was happy to see Tschaikovsky's *Andante Can-
tabile* on the program this afternoon. How beautiful it is! I never tire of it. One hears the Russian
folk-song in the first theme, but in the second it is
Tschaikovsky himself speaking."

Some hours later we were climbing the stone
steps of Noel Sullivan's Hyde Street house. Musicians and their friends were gathered there for
Sunday night supper. Henri Deering met us at the
door and steered the Molinaris up the winding

staircase. Deering was to play the César Franck *Variations Symphoniques* with Molinari on his next program. It was the first meeting between the two artists and the younger man's deference to the older showed in the reverent manner with which he assisted his senior. Lamps were burning before holy shrines in dim hallways through which we walked. They twinkled like lights on a hillside from niches sunk in the curving arm of the walls that followed the spiral lines of the steps. Noel came out of the wide door of the living-room and the chatter within stopped a moment as he greeted us:

"This house was once a convent. It belonged to the Carmelite Order, of which my sister is a member," he explained. "See the alcove above the living-room. On that elevated platform the high altar stood. The house also gets interest from another of its owners," continued Noel. "The family of Robert Louis Stevenson lived here."

"That accounts for the ship models and pictures that decorate some of the rooms," added Deering.

Molinari seated at the long supper table described his home in Rome with its fourteenth-century furnishings. It seems the Molinari family is housed on two floors of an apartment building and their dogs are one of the important features of their ménage. When a particular sister-in-law arrives for a visit she immediately buys canary birds and goldfish. Soon there is mourning in the house, for the birds after a day of incessant song suddenly flop to the bottom of the cage and when inspected they are quite dead. Those familiar with the ways of street vendors assure the Molinaris that the canaries are given some kind of poison which works at the end of a number of hours. The one who has lost the bird returns to the merchant, to whom she relates the catastrophe. In a burst of Italian emotion the bird-seller sympathizes, then offers for sale a new songster which, he vows, will live forever.

"Dozens of these birds come to us and so do many goldfish but we do not have time to become accustomed to them before—pouf!" (Molinari snapped his finger)—"they are finished just like that!"

"Tell me, *Maestro*," suggested Noel, "what men you single out as the leading composers in Italy today?"

"Respighi and Pizetti are among the best of the moderns," replied Molinari.

"Yes, I like Respighi," exclaimed a neighbor of Molinari's eagerly, "because he has melody in his compositions."

"But, Madame," exclaimed Molinari, "all pieces have melody. Melody is only an idea. Music," he continued, "has modes and manners as clothes and furniture have. One hears of Casella writing in two keys, or Ravel's rhythmical style in *Bolero*. These composers are simply showing their musical inventions."

From modern compositions Molinari digressed to speak of famous leaders. "Nikisch," he commented warmly, "was in a class by himself. To watch him and to study the grace, beauty, and intelligence of his hands as he directed was an unforgettable experience. Mahler," added Molinari, "was a spirit of tremendous intellectual force."

With a mischievous smile the little leader from Rome related one of Nikisch's adventures. A performance of *Fidelio* was under way with Nikisch conducting and a trumpeter had been stationed in a courtyard back of the stage. At a certain phrase he was to play a trumpet call. The moment arrived for the blast but no sound came, so Nikisch halted the music and listened, but there was only a deathly stillness. Finally he signaled to the orchestra and the piece was finished without the dramatic touch from behind the scenes. The music over, Nikisch rushed to the courtyard and there discovered the trumpeter pinned and struggling in the arms of two determined gendarmes.

"He wanted to spoil your concert for you, Mister, but we stopped him," called the proud policeman.

After rising from the table Molinari walked to the great window over-looking the garden. The curtain was pulled aside that he might see the vague shadowy outline of a very old statue of St. Francis of Assisi. The leaves and stalks of the garden foliage were white under the moon. A gentle expression on the face of the saint was barely perceptible, but it graced the garden with a loveliness that was divinely tender. Molinari nodded affectionately in the direction of the stone carving— "The greatest Italian of them all," he murmured.

XVII

BRUNO WALTER AND ANTONIA BRICO

THE Philharmonic, now uncontestably established, began to seek material throughout the world. Successive seasons at Woodland Theatre brought us one by one most of the stars who were attracting notice in the large cities of Europe and of our own country. A powerful figure among these and one recognized as an impressive exponent of music was the leader from Berlin, Bruno Walter. We had heard Walter at one concert during our second season when he had made a hurried trip from the Hollywood Bowl to give us a performance. Many requests for his return finally resulted in his accepting an engagement for three concerts with us in 1929, and of course the San Francisco Summer Symphony and the Hollywood Bowl were included in his tour.

Arriving in San Francisco late one evening Walter was spared the usual ceremony of being photographed, except by one wise reporter who had armed his camera-man with flashlights. Madame Walter who accompanied her husband explained their arrival ahead of schedule. Her husband, she said, wanted to avoid starting his work too quickly after their long journey. A severe illness following his first visit to California had decided them to go about things more moderately this time and they were planning to motor on the following day to Del Monte where they would stay until the Tuesday rehearsal.

The orchestra was exhilarated over the return of the leader who had achieved such fine results for them and when Walter stepped upon the platform for his first rehearsal they gave him prolonged applause. His sturdy, strong figure planted very squarely on his feet, gave the signal for Mendelssohn's *Midsummer Night's Dream.*

As I watched Walter I recalled the manners of various conductors upon the stand. It is a matter of speculation as to why they use a certain stance. Each leader gives a different reason for his method of handling the orchestra. Walter says the whole group of players is held together by his standing firmly upon his feet and never moving from his original position after the orchestra is under way. Gabrilowitsch does not think this technique necessary, but says that one must move and be pliable to enforce his ideas, while Molinari argues that the whole of his effects are obtained from his arms and his shoulders, and to emphasize what he means the steel-like muscles are called to witness that it is from the upper part of the body that the governing authority is applied. Artur Rodzinski seems to fire his men by the intense gaze which he continuously pours over them.

"I will tell you what it is," says Rodzinski when questioned about his system with the orchestra. "A conductor is like a military chief in the field. He must know where his men have to be at a certain time; then it is his business to have them there at the appointed moment."

Antonia Brico tells of the way in which she was taught the art of conducting. Her teacher placed the responsibility upon his pupils from the start. The students were put before a mirror. A symphony was then played upon two pianos with the instructor at one of the pianos; the music was conducted by a pupil: If the student gave wrong cues or interpretations those at the pianos played as they had been told to. The effects of mistakes were painful, and when the poor bewildered novice who was leading protested with:

"But, Professor, you know that isn't right. Why do you play it that way?"

The answer was:

"We are only poor players dependent upon your directions."

This was the only method used to teach the student—the teacher never taking the stick to show how it should be done.

Brico thinks that very few realize that there is a technique in conducting just as there is in the playing of any instrument. The leader's task is much more subtle as his instrument is alive and constantly changing as the feelings of the musicians composing the instrument change, so that one can never be certain that the orchestra have finished their preparation for a concert, as one can after so many hours of piano practice.

Discussing rhythm Brico explained:

"In counting four, a one-arm stroke and its sets of muscles are used—not four separate strokes. The orchestra," she commented, "understand immediately whether a conductor knows the technique of his art by the amount that he talks. The silent method is especially valuable where rehearsal time is limited as it is at the Hollywood Bowl."

Chatting on about those famous in her profession, Brico, with her energetic nature, kindled as she praised Karl Muck:

"Although seventy-one years old he is still wonderful in his leadership, full of fire and beauty; and his work has never lost its vivid interpretation or become dry. Too often a conductor is so radical that he takes many liberties with the classics, using them for the exploiting of his own personal mannerisms."

Bruno Walter is certainly unaffected in style. In the Salzburg summer activities he is the genius who leads the Mozart Festival and in May in Covent Garden he gives London its taste of German opera. Like Gabrilowitsch, Walter finds much to interest him in philosophy and world politics. Chinese paintings and poetry and Oriental art in general are among his enthusiasms.

This conductor's logical mind was shown one day while lunching in one of Hollywood's overdecorated hotels. He glanced at the ceiling which was veiled in gauze and studded with stars to imitate the night sky. Having inspected this motley invention for a few moments Walter pensively remarked:

"I can't see why people have to have stars and a moon in the daytime. What kind of a delight does it give them?"

"I suppose the hotel management thinks that the contrast will please," suggested Walter's neighbor at the table. "And besides, isn't it all in keeping with Hollywood's theatrical atmosphere?"

"I don't know about that," Walter answered. "But why not have the room where one eats the noonday meal filled with sunshine and the beautiful reality of the daylight which belongs to the moment. All of this kind of thing presupposes that people are infantile and must be attracted by the kind of entertainment that might amuse children."

The real stars above the Hollywood Bowl, where the symphonies are played at night, were a different matter to Bruno Walter who spoke with deep feeling of the beauty of the music in the still air of the southern skies. Diplomatically he finished his praise of the great Bowl by turning to a visitor from the north who was listening:

"But I love San Francisco and the cool days and the exhilarating ocean winds. Even the fog there is aristocratic!"

We were able to see how effectively Walter could deal with an awkward situation during a concert at the Woodland Theatre. The orchestra was moving along and gaining strength and momentum under the superb treatment given the *Siegfried Idyl*. Under the spell of *Siegfried,* and lost in reveries, we were suddenly brought to an awakening by a low murmur of consternation which rumbled through the theatre. One or two persons rose from their chairs looking as if they were about to dart forward to the stage. The leader and the orchestra, rapt in their task, were unheeding of the unrest about them. Those seated in the audience saw a large brown and white St. Bernard dog making his way up the steps evidently intent upon a tour of investigation to find out what was going on upon the platform. Stifled groans from music lovers mingled with faint giggles from those less perturbed by the thought of a fiasco. There was no usher in sight and no one dared to make what was dreadful enough worse by attempting to stop the ambling St. Bernard.

Piastro has seen the animal and now Penha looks up. A furtive hand from a player is stretched out in a feeble gesture intended to discourage the dog from further explorings. But to no purpose. With wonder in his eyes and with a bushy brown tail waving in the hope of disarming hostility the St.

Bernard walked straight up to Walter and began acquaintanceship by preliminary sniffling. The leader's attention was aroused. With only a glance of command at the animal he attempted to go on with *Siegfried* but the collar, which the big dog wore about his woolly neck was covered with metal buckles and license tags, and a tune of its own jingled out as the wearer trotted about. For a few moments the song of *Siegfried* soared above the song of the brass tags but the solo performer of the canine world seemed to gain over the music in sound and accent. Hopelessly defeated Walter threw down his stick and the orchestral strains slithered off into a wail like children hastily dismissed from school upon an alarm of fire. Men armed with hats and handkerchiefs beat at the St. Bernard who looked at them coolly. Could it be that he was not wanted? He made up his mind that this was the only way in which all of the waving and the urgings of menacing hands could be interpreted and with an air of "all right, if you don't wish me to be here I will be running along" off he trotted down the ravine. Walter waited until the tune of the brass tags had become lost in the banks of the creek before he rapped for attention. Once again *Siegfried* closed in upon our senses and we rushed into the mock world of the gods.

Bruno Walter and all his family are interested in things artistic. The elder daughter is occupied with her career as a singer and her father loves to tell of how he dashes off after one of his own concerts to take an airplane and fly to some European city where she is to appear. Apparently the Germans make much use of the swift transportation afforded them by their fine air lines; Walter says it is the only way to travel and he insists that when the trans-continental air service is perfected it will be a boon to artists who must now spend three days upon a train in order to reach the Pacific Coast.

"Once you have air service," Walter continues, "you will attract all of the great musicians, for every condition here is ideal except the distance which one must travel before he reaches your country."

Apparently the habit of flying is not only a custom of Walter *père,* for on the day of his concert at Hillsborough his youngest daughter arrived with a group of friends from Hollywood via the air route. Her father in talking of her interest in the moving picture life and in jazz music was a little regretful as he deplored the popularity and spread of jazz through Europe. He admitted its quick and captivating effects but thought that its power to hold its own is fleeting, since a piece of music is written for the day and forgotten to-morrow.

"Is it not too bad," commented Walter, "to write stuff that cannot last?"

Jazz was attracting some of the best talent in the orchestra, he admitted. They leave symphony positions to accept places in jazz orchestras. Walter added that he had discovered one of the finest trombone players he knew of anywhere playing in a jazz orchestra. This man had left a first-desk position with a leading symphony organization to take a post in a movie and vaudeville house. When questioned as to his motive for making the change his answer was that he could earn four times as much in his new berth.

To illustrate the trend of to-day Walter played for us Prokofieff's *Symphonie Classique* which amusingly shows the ironic way in which the classics are regarded by our contemporary musicians. In this clever score we hear the complicated and syncopated rhythms attacking and routing the fine old sedate and slow-moving pace of the symphony.

"Will it ever be possible to persuade our young people to love the classics that are written for all time?" wondered the thoughtful conductor. He spoke more on this subject adding with great feeling that if we failed to give these works and to educate our children to love them, certainly we could not hold them responsible for not enjoying the masterpieces.

Bruno Walter loves Mozart music more than any other. As he played for us *Eine Kleine Nachtmusik* we felt how close he was in thought and affection to his favorite composer. How happy he must be at those Salzburg Festivals which are given for the express purpose of perpetuating the genius of Mozart.

XVIII

THE CREATOR OF OPERA IN
SAN FRANCISCO

INTO the city of San Francisco there came a sturdily
built young Neapolitan whose eager, restless spirit
inquired of our people why we did not have any
grand opera in our superb city. This lusty-voiced
stranger pointed to the flower-covered hills of San
Francisco and then his arm swung outward to the
Golden Gate:

"Look!" he said. "Everything of beauty is here
but you have no opera."

We felt abashed and even guilty as if this newcomer had said: "You have a beautiful body but
you have no soul!"

After several groups of people had heard again
and again the comment: that as a city we were unrivalled in the world except for one thing, they
began to talk among themselves and then to approach others to ask:

"Why is it that we who have all this superb
beauty in our natural surroundings have never

thought to match the gifts of nature with a gift
from ourselves? This state of things cannot go on.
We must hurry to get ourselves an opera house and
if it takes too long to build one we must at least
begin with an opera season."

And so the young Neapolitan, whose name was
Gaetano Merola, was invited to make us a plan
and to direct us as to how we might go ahead with
an opera project. In this wise the energetic Italian
aroused San Francisco so that now she not only has
an opera season but her enterprise has fired Los
Angeles with a desire to emulate our achievements,
and she, too, has acquired Merola and his company
of opera stars for a limited series of performances
just following those given in the north. It is almost
incredible that one man should have so inspired
patrons of art, artists, business men, and civic-
minded individuals that these groups finally united
to form an opera association which every year raises
money, sells tickets, and promotes a demand that
occasions sold-out houses.

For final proof of his zeal and devotion to his
profession we must see him night after night in the
orchestra pit during the short and intensive season, gesticulating fervidly to those on the stage and
to the instrumentalists clustered about him as his

brown forelock dangles above his alert brown eyes.

Few rehearsals, new and changing stars, and fresh recruits for the chorus make Merola's task a difficult one and often the results are not as successful as they might be if the director was not hampered by these limitations. But as we watch the ceaseless beat of Merola's baton through endless hours we realize that we are in the presence of a desperately earnest leader.

San Francisco opera has been created on a civic plan. Stars are brought to us from other centres of opera to sing the leading rôles, whereas our chorus is assembled from the chorals and choirs of the city's societies and churches. Housed as the opera was for years in the great Civic Auditorium, where sound was swallowed up by huge draperies festooned as decorations, and where the audience sat upon small and uncomfortable chairs, the success of Merola's plan is a tribute to his indomitable courage.

Bernard Shaw once wisely remarked:

"Get the show and you will get the theatre."

And so it has been with us. For the dogged Neapolitan mind of Merola has hung on to his ideas, pushing on a little more daringly each year into bigger plans until the new War Memorial Opera House has thrown open its great doors to the music devotees and has been pronounced by Olin Downes to be the most perfectly equipped opera house in the world.

The first season in the new opera house was given in the fall of 1932, during days when the financial storm leadened our skies with dark, threatening, impenetrable clouds, but the public streamed to the box office for season seats and soon there were no more to be had. San Francisco partially solved the problem by installing huge amplifiers in the Civic Auditorium where our citizens were invited to listen to broadcasts of the performance free of charge.

Merola whose profession is opera, whose hobby is opera, whose success has been in opera, has too much of the dramatic style to be an excellent conductor of symphony and his technique is too quick and too tense for the *andantes*—those sedately moving numbers in the great symphonies. At a concert in Woodland Theatre we heard him give a program largely made up of excerpts from the operas. Here the suite from *Carmen* and the "March of the Viceroy" from Joseph Redding's and Templeton Crocker's Chinese opera *Fay Yen Fah* permitted an unleashing of the gusto which incites an opera director.

The opera pit is Merola's proper setting, from which, at the close of a performance, he is led by the gracious smiles of Madame Jeritza and the sturdy hand of John Charles Thomas to stand before the cascade-of-gold curtain, where sandwiched between the two stars, in an imposing prominence, he bows to the audience whose applause is far more intense than that usually accorded a leader. For Merola shines as the Inspiration without which there would never have been an opera—or an opera house—in San Francisco.

XIX

ERNEST BLOCH

"I will lift up mine eyes to the hills, from whence cometh my help," intoned Cantor Rindor.

"My help is in the Lord," responded the exultant voices of the choir.

Prayers and psalms ascended, followed by the low notes of an organ surging with the choristers upward towards the dome of the hallway.

"It is very beautiful music," said Ernest Bloch. "Shall we sit here and listen?" he suggested. "They are going to give something of mine soon."

The chanting continued portraying, in the rise and fall of the voices, the pastoral character of the hillsides upon which the flocks of Israel once grazed.

"I am going to tell you something about what music means to the Jewish people," said Cantor Rindor as the first part of the program closed with a psalm. "Perhaps you do not know that Jewish people have folk-songs and that they sing them over and over to each new generation. Particularly in the East where the Jewish population keep so much to themselves are these folk-tunes kept alive. Like the prayers and the reading of the scriptures, the songs are given in a sing-song voice. In this way the people learn to sing half-tones and quarter-tones and this habit of expressing themselves in song probably accounts for the fine ear that many of the Jews possess."

"The Jewish mother," continued Rindor, "sings to her child, and it is while singing that she whispers to him of her dreams that he may grow up to be a good rabbi, or a great man in some walk of life. I remember one folk-song in which a rabbi is heard teaching the children, who are sitting by his hearth, to sing the Hebrew consonants and vowels. Jewish people use music not just occasionally as a vehicle for their thoughts and emotions, and not only in religion, while they praise God and bewail their sins, but they sing where other people would speak."

"Ernest Bloch," remarked Rindor, "is represented on this program with *Baal Shem,* three pictures of Chassidic life. This work will tell you better than I can the meaning music has for our people."

"Piastro is to play my *Baal Shem* on his violin,"

Bloch whispered to me. "Please listen particularly to the first picture called 'Contrition.' You will hear the wailing and lamenting in a minor key similar to the Gregorian Chant. Later in the composition comes the major key—wherein one feels that liberation and peace have reached the soul."

At the close of the concert Bloch talked of his symphonic work *America* which he had recently conducted in Woodland Theatre.

"I led the piece also in Amsterdam," he said, "and I had a chorus of one hundred voices who sang the words of the anthem in English. Mengelberg appreciated my composition but he told me that it would take another twenty-five years for the world to realize its merit."

Later Bloch remarked, with some pathos, to a group of acquaintances:

"I am leaving the San Francisco Conservatory, you know, and my plans are very much in the air although the University of California is giving me an annuity for several years so that I may be free to write. This sum," remarked Bloch somewhat in the grand manner, "will keep me in a modest way."

"How do you feel about leaving us, Mr. Bloch?" asked a dark-haired beauty who wore the traditional costume of a Jewess of ancient times that

we might feel pictorially the rich, sumptuous quality of the early life of the race.

Bloch's eyes traveled over the colored silks on
the tunic of this modern *Judith* and he answered
slowly with a far-away look:

"I love the people of California. But there is no
one here that I can talk to, or with whom I can
exchange ideas. I am starved for companionship
and do not know whether to stay on in California
or go abroad."

"I am an American," he continued, "and I have
taken out my citizen papers but now I may go back
to Geneva."

"Would you care to do that, Mr. Bloch?" asked
the young woman he was addressing.

"I do not know," Bloch replied. "I left Geneva
when I was thirty-six years old upon the advice
of friends and came to America. The people in
Geneva did not understand me."

"How do you feel about the future of the Conservatory?" inquired one of the group which had
gathered around to listen.

"They have done much there and Miss Ada
Clement and Miss Lilian Hodgehead can never
be adequately thanked for all their efforts. I am
dedicating one of my most important works to

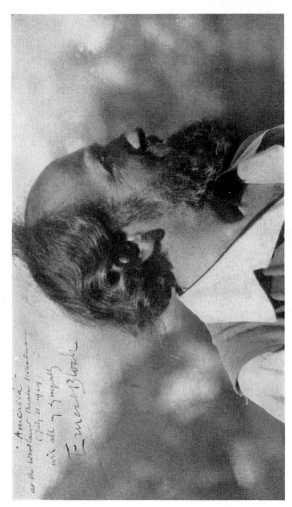

Ernest Bloch

them as they have made it possible for me to accomplish something here. The orchestra at the Conservatory is not large enough to do much, particularly in the larger works," commented Bloch. "I had hoped to build it up to full size. With all that I had in me I talked and talked to the people of San Francisco—hoping to wake them up musically —but they did not seem to hear me. It was like speaking to a blank wall. My audiences simply did not listen. But then," Bloch remarked, "people are only interested along lines which best serve their self-interest."

"Oh! I don't agree with you entirely," interrupted the young beauty. "I think that people usually have reasons for what they do."

"Do you?" returned Bloch. "Now I think that love is always the same."

"Yes, but motives may be different," insisted the stately "Judith."

Bloch's strong, lean, brown hands moved ceaselessly as he talked. He seemed to be tapping out a rhythm to some unsounded melody, while his voice, soft and womanish, was an ineffectual medium for his perturbed thought.

In appearance and manners Bloch is of the East India type and had his thin, soft, dark hair been permitted to grow long he might easily be mistaken for a Cingalese.

Again he spoke:

"Many persons think that a knowledge of harmony is all that is necessary in order to compose music. We must also have ideas, as harmony without ideas is of no avail." Bloch smiled at "Judith's" eager face.

"It is kind of Mrs. Marcus Koshland to have us here to-day at her lovely home—to hear the Hebrew songs and to find sympathetic companionship. I have antennae," he said in a low voice, "and they tell me how sympathetic and understanding you are. They are terrible things, these antennae, for most often they bring me pain." "Judith" moved uneasily as Bloch looked at her with his searching gaze.

More guests crowded towards us and I detached myself from Bloch and his coterie to chat for a moment with the Redfern Masons. In a few casual words I asked Mrs. Mason why I had not seen her for some time. She commenced some explanation but was stopped by her husband who said quickly:

"I can tell you why you don't see more of her. It is because you are not a sub-normal, Chinese

child and Mrs. Mason does not see any other kind
of people. She seems to think that all the moron
Chinese children are her especial possessions and
even I cannot compete with them."

XX

HENRY EICHEIM AND HIS TEMPLE BELLS

THE workshop of Henry Eicheim in Santa Barbara is as well supplied with bronze bells and gongs as any well-equipped Buddhist temple. Touching these cups or plaques of metal with a softly padded stick, Eicheim invites his visitor to listen as the overtones of the gongs die away into a thin thread of tone. The trained ear of Eicheim, composer of *Oriental Impressions,* can hear the ringing of the bells long after the less acute senses of the unaccustomed listener have lost the trail of brazen sound.

Eicheim speaks of the "tonal fabric" of his music.

"It is woven," he explains, "from the clang of temple bells—the chanting of a Buddhist priest— the singing of street peddlars."

"In Korea and Siam I used to go to my window attracted there by the cries that I heard in the street below. Strange voices of natives coming from far-away and shrill whistles used by the blind who pattered by with tapping canes fascinated me. When I tried to reproduce their sounds with their quarter and sixteenth tones, nothing imitated their true character. I grew interested and puzzled, and determined to catch those illusive little tunes and put them on paper, I tried to get what I wanted on my violin, and then the native instruments came to my help."

"Here are photographs of the temples which house the sacred chimes. Those figures on that altar are gilded idols. The headdresses are magnificent. Look at the long pointed metal-tipped finger nails."

The Eicheims had recorded their sight-seeing by taking many pictures of subjects which most appealed to them. They had snap-shots by the hundreds of the pagodas and lacquered gates that assist the Orientals in ministering to their gods.

Eicheim explains his manner of using the gongs by walking to the piano, after he has set a wave of sound hammering through the air, and striking upon the keyboard a note which corresponds to the tone of the vibrating gong. Next he has to search out the overtones to express the ideas that he wishes to use for his effects.

"Do you hear those harmonics? They are wonderful. That is F natural that is sounding now."

From the Eicheim studio we walked out into their lovely garden with its background of dark, fir-covered mountains. The half-savage clang of the gongs followed us like ghost-sounds as if the Eicheims had captured some strange spirit in their Malayan travels and had brought it home to Santa Barbara where his voice cried out in loneliness for his own kind through the dusk that spread over the valley.

XXI

WALTER DAMROSCH

THE many talents of Walter Damrosch scintillated as, one by one, they were pressed into service when he conducted summer symphony concerts in California.

Dr. and Mrs. Damrosch traveled from New York to San Francisco by way of Santa Barbara.

"My daughter Polly, who married Sidney Coe Howard, the playwright, is living in the South," explained Damrosch as he stepped from the Pullman which brought him north for his engagements. "And my wife and I were largely influenced to come west by our desire to see Polly and her husband. I left Mrs. Damrosch with our daughter but they will both be here for my opening concert in Hillsborough."

While driving to the St. Francis Hotel, where he was to stay, Damrosch chatted on:

"I have conducted here before, you know. The last time was in 1916 when I led for Margaret Anglin who gave plays in the Greek Theatre. You have a reputation in California for being a state that produces many geniuses. Numbers of people, celebrated in the musical world, have come from here, and that reminds me: What of Maud Fay? Is she living in San Francisco?"

"Yes, indeed! And waiting to talk over old Munich days with you," replied one of the group which was escorting Damrosch to his hotel. "Maud is planning a moonlight supper party for you up on Mt. Tamalpais where the people of Marin County have built themselves a fine clubhouse."

Damrosch smiled broadly:

"I remember Fay singing for me in San Francisco," he continued, "when I was asked to give my opinion of her talent for opera. What a gorgeous creature she was; and her voice was rich and very sympathetic."

"Your city is famous for singers and also for its Bohemian life and its good food. I am a good cook myself and I know how your chefs excel in their profession. To return to music," interrupted Damrosch, who "who is to be my concert-master?"

"Piastro," replied our manager.

"That is splendid! And when and where do we rehearse?"

"In the Knights of Columbus Hall at nine-thirty to-morrow morning. Walter Oesterreicher our concert manager will call for you."

The big, pleasant-faced man walked away with a brisk step into the St. Francis where he was planning to spend the day in arranging the extensive program which awaited his sanction.

The power of the radio was demonstrated in all its amazing strength, through the many channels it provided for reaching the people during the days before the Damrosch *première*. A stream of publicity poured out over the National Broadcast System which sought to get the ear of Damrosch fans and to whet their curiosity for a glimpse of the celebrity. The N.B.C. had wired Woodland Theatre for a nation-wide hook-up and the Damrosch concerts were to be broadcast throughout the United States. It was a significant event in the history of radio as no orchestra transmitting from the Pacific Coast had ever been heard in the East. Our friends in New York had been notified of the exact hour when they should tune in and get that thrill which always attends a first venture of any kind.

Damrosch was the central thought in thousands of minds. Persons who had been deaf to our plea to buy tickets streamed into the office of the Philharmonic where they purchased seats for the Damrosch performance that they might see in person the man who had aroused their enthusiasm as he talked to them on the air.

"I don't know anything about music," said the merchant from the hardware shop, next door to our office, as he bought his tickets, "but I have listened to that man talk for so many years that I want to see what he looks like."

"Will he speak to us before he begins the concert?" asked other patrons. "Please get him to say just a few words."

Our city was alive with musicians and those interested in promoting the art during these days in June as the Federation of Women's Clubs headed by their president, Mrs. Elmer Ottoway, and watched over by the radiant spirit of Mrs. Edgar Stillman Kelley, was holding a meeting in San Francisco. Damrosch had been asked to officiate as master of ceremonies at the presentation of the prize which the Federation was offering for a special symphonic work commemorating the occasion, and he was afterward to play the composition at one of the summer symphony concerts in the Civic Auditorium.

In these many appearances, all of which exacted

tact, wit, and an ability to rise to the occasion, the great man never faltered or failed to satisfy his admirers. The crowd thrilled to the famous voice that carried in its slow phrases a combination of Anglo-Saxon broad vowels spiced with Teutonic gutterals. Audiences would not be satisfied until Damrosch had spoken to them and they listened to him like people who had been hungry for bread and who were being fed at last. It was something like watching a conjuror at work, for everything about Damrosch, and particularly his looks and his voice, mesmerized his adoring public. They called him back to the stage again and again not only to show their undivided approval but, moved by the desire to study him for as long a time as possible, to hold him before the microphone. It was astonishing to watch the power of this personality; for Damrosch seemed to be a special messenger from some source of comfort, and in the bright spotlight he stood while his worshippers adored him. Such homage must be a sure support and a potent stimulus to the efforts of a star conductor such as Walter Damrosch.

XXII

THE IRISH COMPOSER-CONDUCTOR:
SIR HAMILTON HARTY

"My sister and I used to attend the county fairs in Ireland and it was there that I picked up the tunes that you hear in my *Irish Symphony*."

There was a mischievous smile upon Sir Hamilton Harty's ruddy face and his eyes were bright with memories as he told of the street scenes in his native County Down.

"On Fair days," Harty reminisced, "the town was filled with people dancing to joy tunes and penny whistles. With my tongue fastened about a bit of sticky, yellow jacket that was warranted to 'draw the teeth out of ye' I followed the fakirs and the jugglers, or I hung about Fat Charlie with his cart of herrings. Somehow I managed to get into all the little side shows. It was the greatest fun. The songs I heard kept running about in my mind; I whistled them; I sang them; finally I put them on paper."

"All my boyhood is in the *Irish Symphony*," explained Sir Hamilton, while he looked shyly at us with a hesitating expression as if he feared that his confidences might be too naive. The wondering look in his eyes must have been part of his youthful make-up. It was easy to picture the youngster dodging along the curved roadways in and out between the heavy figures of the grown-ups while his tune-loving ear picked up the melody of "The Girl I Left Behind Me," which was played with fervor by the village band.

"Was all your early life lived in Ireland, Sir Hamilton?" asked a woman who was seated on a low couch with the conductor.

Sir Hamilton lit a cigarette before replying quietly:

"Yes, all my early life. My parents were very poor. All Ireland is poor. We were a big family and we had such hard times to take care of everybody. My father brooded a great deal over our slavery which was the result of our poverty, but my mother—she was the only one for whom life seemed perfect and complete. She had brought her children into the world and that was what she was on earth to do. She was like a queen and moved regally about in our house wholly because she had been successful in her own life. But my father always craved liberty and he felt that no one ever could arrive at his goal until he was unhampered by the responsibilities and the cares that kill the spirit. He often talked to me of how cruelly our existence, ground out in want, crushed the finest in every man. And I believe that myself," said Harty emphatically. "To live and to be happy and to give one's best, one must be free to seek what he needs that he may be stimulated to do his *best* work."

"Isn't that a dangerous philosophy for the major part of humanity, Sir Hamilton?" queried his neighbor.

"No, we only think so because we have not found out the way to free ourselves. We are still slaves of old tradition," asserted Harty with warm feeling. But why talk of these sad things when your California is so beautiful and you American women are so disarmingly frank and, may I say, disconcertingly delightful?"

"Why are we disconcerting?" asked a young woman perched on a big rose-velvet-covered chair near the leader.

"Because you are frank, dear lady. In an American woman's eyes there is no consciousness that she is intended to be the object of man's conquest."

"But we don't feel that way towards our men," answered the young woman. There was a wistfulness in her eyes as she spoke which indicated that there was a certain dangerous appeal in Sir Hamilton's idea of what a woman should be thinking of when she found herself engaged in a *tête-à-tête* with a stalking male.

"Tell me, Sir Hamilton," continued the occupant of the rose-colored chair, "what should a woman do if she is not to be frank?"

"Oh," Harty answered laughingly, "an American woman cannot do anything but what she does. Her men see to that by the adoration and homage which they pay her and the pedestal on which they place her, but with a European woman it is different. She makes a man feel that he is paying court to her and there is always the idea in his mind that he is in the presence of, shall I say, something very alluring, dangerous, and feminine."

"No!" his little neighbor answered shyly, "we are not like that."

That enchanted haze which is reputed to envelop Ireland and her people surrounds Sir Hamilton, although he is far from Erin's shore. Unreality stirs his imagination and a curiosity about the phenomena of the unseen world engrosses his thoughts. This mystic trend of his philosophy carries him into an acceptance of spiritism. As Harty is a cousin of the famous palmist, Count Hamon, otherwise known as Cheiro, it is probable that in his family lies a strong urge towards the occult. Their belief seems to represent a struggle against realism. Perhaps it arises from a hatred of the limitations that encompass our ordinary modes of living and is only a defense against that which seems to them painfully ugly. Perhaps it was the elder Harty's counsel to his son to escape from law and tradition into an untrammeled world that has caused the composer to be attracted towards spirit revelations which are bursting with dramatic interest coming, as they do, with the significance of sights that baffle our comprehension. It may well be that, in associating himself with the magic of the unknown, Sir Hamilton Harty is following his own creed "to live and to be happy, and to give one's best one must be free to seek what he needs *when* he needs it."

XXIII

MONSIEUR AND MADAME MONTEUX

THE principal number chosen for the Monteux introductory program was Rimsky-Korsakoff's ballet pantomime *Sheherezade.* Monteux first came to America in 1916, to make a transcontinental tour with the Russian ballet. After this he conducted French opera at the Metropolitan, going from this post to Boston, where he held the position of Director with the Boston Symphony for five years. The renown won by Monteux for his interpretation of the ballet had whetted our desire to hear him lead the musical setting for the magic tales from the Arabian Nights. Piastro's pure tone glowed in the song of the Princess to meet the *arpeggios* Kajetan Attl's lean brown fingers plucked from his gold harp. The audience forgot its self-restraint and—moved by the polished elegance of Monteux and the playing of the two artists—they burst into cheers as the dancing rhythms rushed forth from the instruments like flames from gigantic open fires.

Throughout his concert the bright black eyes of Monteux traveled searchingly and ceaselessly over each section of the orchestra they responded to his beat with clamoring drums and clinking tambourines.

"Watch the men's faces as Monteux smiles at them," whispered Dean Sellards. "They look as if they were face to face with a god."

Pierre Monteux and his sprightly wife were as enlivening in their conversation as the golden champagne of their native France. Monteux, who resembles a glorified cupid, seems to be on the best of terms with life. At the corners of his mouth half hidden by his pointed, turned-up mustache are two short curved lines which suggest laughter, and at the outer edge of his extremely bright dark eyes are small creases which show that laughter lies not only upon his lips but that it sparkles through the core of his being. There is an infectious quality in the good humor of Monteux and his wife which affects those who engage them in a *tête-à-tête* or listen to their amusing anecdotes.

Madame Monteux is charmingly unrestrained in her speech. In social affairs the boredom that sometimes settles upon a function is frequently the result of company manners and too much restraint of conversation. An inconsequential, naive remark, however, brings a fearless spirit into the lifeless atmosphere, and the paralysis that had frozen the wits and tongues of the guests is suddenly routed. I can still hear Madame Monteux speaking to a group of strangers:

"What do you think of this jacket I am wearing?" she asks while her glance travels appealingly to her audience.

"It's great," answers a masculine voice speaking with undue emphasis caused by the happy escape into trivial things.

"Yes, indeed!" echo the others. "It is perfectly charming.

"Do you think so?" questions Madame Monteux with a strange little pucker ruffling her brow usually so smooth. "I don't think so at all. I think it is hideous but Pierre likes me to wear it as it protects my arms."

A little gasp interrupts her candor, but she speaks on unheeding the effect of her words.

"Pierre!" she calls towards the corner where Monteux is gesticulating as he tells some fiery anecdote to his coterie. "Pierre! I am just telling these good people that you make me cover up my arms with this ugly little jacket."

Now, strange as it may seem, this personal exposure of a domestic secret between Monteux and his wife does not apparently offend anyone. Taken, as we are, into the bosom of the family we are immediately disarmed and we begin to wonder whether it is Monsieur or Madame who is in the right about the small coat. The exposure of Madame's arms seems to play no part in our speculation, but the right of Monteux to envelop his lady in a covering which she dislikes is all important.

As may be easily imagined when we said "Goodnight" to Monsieur and Madame Monteux we felt closer to them than we did to many of the people with whom we have mingled for years.

Again our guests showed their human qualities when Monsieur's watch was taken from the dressing-room of the hall in which we were rehearsing. As intermission was sounded Monteux walked off to get his coat and in a moment appeared, with blanched face.

"My watch!" he whispered to me. "It is gone!"

As I beckoned hastily to the orchestra manager I questioned Monteux in the meantime.

"Where did you leave it?" I asked.

"On the table, by my coat," he replied while his eyes looked piteously into mine.

"I would not grieve so, Madame, but it was a present to me from my orchestra in Paris and for years it has always been with me. I value that testimonial very highly, Madame, and it will sadden me too much to lose it."

"Poor Pierre!" sighed his little wife. "What a pity! Poor, poor Pierre!"

"Lock the doors of the hall!" called out the orchestra manager to the janitor who was lurking, as janitors seem to have a way of doing, just half inside the doorway.

"I will send for the police at once," the manager assured Monteux.

We huddled in the aisle and in silence looked at one another. Soon we were surrounded by detectives.

Could Monsieur swear that he had not forgotten the watch and left it in his hotel room? This was highly probable.

Yes, Monsieur and Madame—who was in tears—could swear that they had started off from the hotel with the watch in its accustomed place.

"Well," advised the detective, "we will search this place but as the exits all gave on to the street, and as all of them are unlocked, whoever took the watch must have slipped in while you people were playing and then got away without anyone seeing him escape."

"Poor Pierre!" was Madame's only answer to this. In fact it was the only answer to this sinister incident; for the watch, with the cherished inscription, never again lay in the fond caressing hand of the kindly *Maestro*.

Monteux upon the podium is another person from the jovial, easy-going guest who allows himself to be shepherded about by hostesses, and, as his heels click in military fashion for the first up-flick of the baton, his bearing is dignified and authoritative. France has an able representative in the genial person of Pierre Monteux.

XXIV

ENRIQUE ARBOS

ENRIQUE ARBOS, leader of the Madrid Symphony, changed many of our previous conceptions of Spanish music when he played Granados' intermezzo from the opera *Goyescas* and the Arbos arrangement of the Albeniz suite *Iberia*. The Spaniards were revealed as having something in their art outside the hysterically dramatic music in which gesture and energy are the pronounced characteristics. Joaquin Turina's gorgeous processions, marching to the accompaniment of a festival chorus whose chanting is broken occasionally by the crash of strident cymbals, show a side of the Spanish temperament at variance with our previous ideas that have been formed largely by listening to *habaneros* and *boleros*. The poetic melancholy and pastoral simplicity which permeate the work of Granados lifts his music high above the coarser expressions of melody accompanied by castenets and tambourines. In hearing Turina and

Granados we feel a deep pathos underlying the song.

Although, upon arrival in California, Arbos was suffering from a severe attack of neuritis, he labored strenuously at rehearsals despite sleepless nights that left him wan and pale. The orchestra was not familiar with the Spanish music and in order to achieve results careful study of the scores was necessary. Through these tedious sessions Arbos conducted with the left arm. Sympathetically-minded new acquaintances offered the neuritis victim all sorts of advice as to how to cure his ailment. Osteopathy, chiropractic treatment and mud baths came up for discussion. It seemed that almost everyone had suffered from the disease and each of the afflicted championed a pet remedy.

Naturally much of the social entertainment planned for the guests from Madrid was abandoned. However, Stanford University presented them to the neighborhood at a luncheon arranged by Dean Sellards. Tables for the guests were placed through the aisles of the cloisters where their colored clothes and centrepieces of gay flowers gave a touch of frivolity to the scholastic surroundings. Waitresses, dressed in green linen smocks, served the company, and as they waited upon the celebrities they gave each one a veiled but close scrutiny.

Arbos, himself an expression of the vital spirit of his race, told us anecdotes in the manner of a true comedian. At times his gentle voice racing in a swift flow of conversation, dropped to a low pitch that bore a ring of precision and authority.

"You should be with me when I take my orchestra into the little hill towns of my country," remarked Arbos to his host. "The whole population turns out to receive us. They come to the village where we are to play from miles distant and their reverent attitude while listening to us is very impressive."

Dean Sellards followed Arbos' descriptions closely.

"What an unusual thing," he exclaimed, "for people who hear so little symphonic music to get so much out of it."

"No," was the answer. "Such people make a fine audience. They do not have any other chance to listen to these works and a visit from our orchestra is for them a great occasion."

"What music do they hear ordinarily?" asked Dean Sellards.

"Their own folk-tunes and dance music, and the real gypsy songs which are very effective as they are streaked with savage emotions. One can never get a correct idea of Spain traveling through it as the tourist usually does," explained Arbos. "It is necessary to go off into the mountains and villages where the people are different from those in the cities."

Arbos was asked if he had always lived in Spain.

"Yes," he replied, "and I studied there as a small boy. The violin was my instrument."

The leader's eyes twinkled in amusement and he was silent for a moment, then said:

"I remember an occasion when, as a child, I played before our Queen. After I had performed she called me to her and asked me what she might give me to show her appreciation of my entertainment."

" 'Your Majesty,' I answered, 'I have often watched you driving by and I have wondered to myself whether I would ever be permitted to sit in your carriage with you. So if it is not too much of a favor to ask I would like to ride with you some day.' "

"The Queen," Arbos continued, "embraced me and promised to gratify my wish, and shortly after this episode I found myself seated at her side in a very high voiture which she was driving. We were off! The Queen prided herself upon her skill with the reins and she was not going to cheat me of any of the thrills which always attended her little journeys. She cracked her whip and constantly touched the four horses with its lash. The pace grew more swift as the Queen's spirit rose to the excitement of her favorite pastime. Perhaps she was performing for the little boy who had played his violin for her."

Dean Sellards smiled as he moved a chair for Madame Arbos who glanced at her husband with the affection she unfailingly bestowed upon him.

"Finish your story," she urged, "and tell about the end of the drive."

Arbos took up the narrative again. "My legs," he said, "were dangling about in the air; my hat was clutched in one hand while with the other hand I clung to the seat beneath me. The carriage rattled and swayed and my childish form pitched and tossed like a wisp of hay in a high wind. Suddenly the Queen turned a sharp corner and down I went on the floor where I finished the drive half buried in the voluminous skirts of my sovereign. When the drive was over and I was asked how I had enjoyed it I could not say that I had spent the time with no view at all except that of the yards of silk draperies spread about me. In a confused way I thanked the Queen and said I had admired so much the billowy scenery."

The calm beauty of Madame Arbos was unruffled by the curious looks which were cast her way. She walked through the Stanford courtyards with a grace that seemed old world among the rapid strides of the Americans clustering about her. An alert and amiable expression in her eyes was the dominant characteristic of features that were clear-cut and patrician.

Senor Arbos was always close to his wife, who cared for him with much concern and affection. Apparently he enjoyed the interest he excited by his illness as he did not become irritable when coaxed into extra scarfs, or an overcoat, by his attentive companion.

Neuritis was ignored or forgotten at the first Arbos concert. With zest and fire the little leader stepped upon the stage. His wax-like skin had taken on a brighter tinge, while his neatly trimmed beard and upturned mustache seemed to announce that we were in the presence of an invincible authority. Arbos' black eyes glittered across the audience which settled to the task of trying to fathom the personality before them.

The Arbos method of conducting was unique. Never seeming to implore his men in order to gain his effects, he stood before them almost indifferently while he accented rhythms by rising on his toes and lifting himself up, time after time, as if he were about to spring into the air. How the orchestra knew what he wanted of them was a mystery, but in that subtle communion which goes on between the musicians and their leader was a perfect understanding of what all the gymnastics intended to convey. Perhaps the spirit of the gorgeous dance tunes never could have been impressed upon the orchestra in any other way.

The Spanish music revived the memory that Spain and California were one in early history. A close kinship between the distant lands was expressed in the varying themes of the compositions played by Arbos. The melodic ideas of Spanish quick steps and whirlpool rhythms interspersed with swinging chimes, was identical with the music which California treasures from the days of Cabrillo. Spain's fingers shaped the early customs of California; her industries transplanted to the shores of the Pacific survive in the olive groves and the wine-presses. Although her dream of conquest and rule of the new world ended in broken fragments, yet upon the highways hang the mission bells for the purpose of directing the traveler upon his journey. The dust of the road once pressed by the feet of monks who traveled up and down the Peninsula has given way to asphalt but the missions are with us! Their brown and gold beauty is fading softly under the weight of their years.

XXV

EUGENE GOOSENS

TALL, poetic-looking Eugene Goosens arrived from England to conduct for us. The Goosens opera *Judith* had just had its *première* in London and the composer had delayed his journey across the Atlantic in order that he might lead the first public appearance of his work. Rushing at once to prepare the orchestra for his first concert Goosens commenced rehearsing Stravinsky's *Petrouchka.*

The aristocratic figure of the young conductor —clad in London's latest fashion of brown flannels and an orange-colored sport shirt—was given a final note of distinction by the silk necktie that blended perfectly with the whole color scheme. Our orchestra could be seen unobtrusively studying these effects as the leader swung his long legs over the tall stool from which he directed the rehearsal. One cannot help remarking Gene Goosens' clothes. The black silk stock of his formal dress denotes fondness for the picturesque cos-

tumes that illustrious artists wore in the nine-
teenth century.

In contrast to the distinguished apparel of the
visitor from London are the often haphazard costumes of many of our prominent artists. Gabrilowitsch tells of the misgivings that torment his
tailor owing to Gabrilowitsch's habit of giving an
order for several suits of clothes—which he ar-
ranges to fit on at a date in the near future—and
then promptly the clothes and the fittings are forgotten and the Director has no recollection of the
transaction until his next visit to New York. Perhaps this may be made a year later, and when Gabrilowitsch sails blythely into the tailor's shop and
begins to select new patterns for suits, the tailor
meekly asks:

"But, Mr. Gabrilowitsch, when are you coming
in to try on the grey suit and the white serge that
you ordered of me this time last year?"

According to Gabrilowitsch his tailor is more
than just a tailor. He is a valued critic and friend,
for he undertakes to see that Gabrilowitsch and
Harold Bauer, who is also a patron, are correctly
turned out when their joint recital for two pianos is
given in New York. A complimentary ticket brings
the costumer to the concert hall where he is deter-

mined to assist his friends and clients to make a pleasing effect upon the audience. One of the earliest to arrive at the concert hall the tailor seats himself in the front row just under the keyboards of the pianos.

"When we walk on to the stage," relates Gabrilowitsch, "we know just where we will find him and we always stand for a moment before beginning the first number while he casts his eye over us searching for any possible mistakes in the details of our clothes and in how they are worn. We are very serious and very still as his gaze travels over our lapels, coat-tails, and the creases of our trousers. Always the tailor raises an eyebrow in disdain, and by putting his hand on his own shoulder he indicates, as he looks pointedly at one or the other of us, just where we have failed in the proper adjustment of his garments. Finally with a shrug which says plainly:

"Well, don't blame me if the recital is not a success; I have done the best I can for you," he drops his eyes to his program and this for us is the signal for the concert to begin.

Bruno Walter's contribution to dress for the stage includes a very elegantly designed, embroidered waistcoat of greyish black silk with small

white scrolls curving ostentatiously through its
lustreful depths. This waistcoat is eloquent of
important occasions. We can imagine Walter, sum-
moned by royalty for a private performance, donning the ceremonious vest which showed his appreciation of the honor conferred upon him.

Problems of conductors' apparel did not seem
to disturb Goosens at all as he forged into the intricate rhythms of the scenes from *Petrouchka*
which tell of the affairs of the puppets. To the
crowd about his booth Petrouchka, the lovesick
doll, was heard declaiming his passion for the Bal-
lerina while the grinding of street organs and the
grunting of a huge performing bear furnished
some of the action for a carnival in full swing about
the puppet show.

"It is necessary to study the modern music as
a subject by itself," Goosens explained a little
later, "for a whole new system is at the root of
these compositions and we have to forget all the
old maps and study the new charts if we are to
find our way through the musical problems of the
present day."

The younger generation does not seem to have
any prejudice against the dissonances and poly-
tonalities which are so distressing to those who are

attuned to diatonic scales. They respond to de Falla and Stravinsky with requests for more of such numbers to be included in our program, while the conservative protest with:

"We can't make it out at all. What are these fellows driving at? This music of theirs doesn't get us anywhere."

From shopkeepers—whose sales of phonograph records are stimulated through the playing of modern works by the symphony orchestra—comes hearty appreciation of the courage of the Philharmonic in giving the debatable compositions:

"Boys and girls love the new works," explained a clerk in the record department of an important music store. "I have often tried to persuade them to buy classical records when they ask my help in their selections, but the answer is:

" 'Oh, those things bore me to death. Give me some hot dance tunes.' However, it is different with *Petrouchka* and Gershwin's *American in Paris*. Albums of these works were in demand after they were played at your concerts."

Henri Deering is another artist in sympathy with contemporary musical thought. At our informal supper parties following the concerts, Goosens and Deering would seat themselves at the

piano and, with a great deal of good-natured jib-
ing at one another's sight-reading, play through
the four-hand scores of Schubert and Beethoven
symphonies. Later on Deering played us a charming Ravel waltz, Griffes' *White Peacock* and Debussy's *Arabesque*. After the volume and majestic
effect of the orchestra the piano sounded like an
ineffectual voice attempting to sing before a crowd.
Only gradually did the tones of the piano gather
in power and intimate beauty so that those of us
who listened were under the spell of music in another guise.

As Deering's mood strayed into the Ravel, Goosens' words hovered in my thoughts:

"It is necessary to study the modern material as
a subject by itself and to forget the old maps if
we are to find our way through the music of to-
day."

XXVI

THE TRISTAN OF THE ORCHESTRA

Artur Rodzinski is often called the "Tristan" of the orchestra world. His sensitive face with its drooping mouth is too sad for the youth which he represents in a field where men do not arrive at distinction until years have seasoned their labor.

Brown eyes hidden by glasses and shoulders habitually bowed are the marks which betoken the student in Rodzinski, while the artist in the man is to be seen in the expressive features which register his moods swiftly and delicately. In Rodzinski's eyes all the trouble and joy in his soul can be read without difficulty, for he never attempts to conceal his feelings. Deep melancholy often plunges him into a dejection from which he extricates himself with difficulty.

When at work the serious side of Rodzinski's nature is to the fore. There is no vagueness or dreaminess in the spirit with which he approaches the preparation of a performance. Always keyed up until a concert is under way this young conductor spends the moments before the opening number sitting thoughtfully and quietly in his dressing room while he studies a photograph of his father which portrays the elder Rodzinski in the uniform of the army of Poland.

"My father is my inspiration," he quickly explains.

"My mother still lives in Poland," he adds, "and I am sending for her to come out to be with me this summer. I cannot meet her in New York and so I shall have a courier look after her and put her on the train. It will all seem very strange to her," Rodzinski comments smilingly, "but she will soon become accustomed to American ways."

"By the way, did you know that the women of Poland are not called by the same name that the men in their families use. My mother is Rodzinska while I am Rodzinski."

"Are your family coming north to hear your concerts?" asked a visitor to the green room.

"Yes, the last one. Mrs. Rodzinski and my son Vidor will come for that. I have a present for the boy for which he has been begging. What do you think it is?"

"A toy airplane," suggested Piastro the concert

manager who stood in a doorway strumming little pizzicato notes on his fiddle.

"No," laughed Rodzinski. "Some Mexican jumping beans. I was telling Vidor about these curiosities which I saw in the window of a Japanese store on my last visit to San Francisco and since then he has not given me a moment's peace."

"Three o'clock, Mr. Rodzinski. Concert starts in two minutes," informs the concert manager.

"So! I am ready," replies the conductor.

Away from his work Rodzinski discards his maturity and enjoys the society of young persons. He often entertains a coterie with card tricks, or by showing them a puzzle ring which he wears on one of his strong well-shaped hands. The design of the ring is formed by two coiled serpents so intricately twisted together that only the initiated can combine the gold wires once they are separated. Rodzinski watches with interest and offers assistance as curious fingers attempt to interlock the grooves of the ring, and when the trinket is handed back to him by defeated contestants he swiftly slips the strands into place.

"So," he remarks quietly; then he urges: "Now you try again."

Invariably after a short period of relaxation Rodzinski returns to his scores. Finding him apart from the crowd of guests who had surrounded him at the swimming pool for an *al fresco* luncheon, I saw that he was studying the pages of Stravinsky's *Sacre du Printemps*.

"Look!" he comments admiringly as his blue pencil pointed out the difficult and intricate rhythms.

"What do blue squares and triangles mean?" I asked.

"Those," he explained, "I make to show where I divide the bar. Watch now," he continued. "Here I count two, then three for five-eighths, and here three, then three again for six-eighths. This method simplifies the rhythm."

"Stravinsky is sometimes referred to as only a mathematical genius but look at these pages (Rodzinski turned the leaves) . Here," he said, "you will see the great inspiration."

While talking, the leader's white teeth, which are his flawless asset in looks, gleam through a rare smile that music only coaxes to his melancholy features. He brushes his hands through his thick, curly, brown hair; then bends more intently to

Orchestra and Guests at Mrs. Armsby's Swimming-Pool

peer into his book, and again he begins to explain his technique:

"When I count a beat of two," he said, "I go down; then up like this." Rodzinski took my hand and guided it through the air. As my arm moved he corrected me: "Never a straight line, always move in a curve and sweep your hand as you count."

I followed his lead.

"My arm swings like a cradle," I exclaimed.

"That is right," he nodded, "and now I will show you how to count four. See, I go one to the right, then up, then an oblique line, then back. Never go down but once in a bar," he continued. "It confuses the orchestra. Go anywhere after you have finished your count—up, and up again, as far as you need to—but don't go down."

"Your questions make me think," remarked Rodzinski, "of the need there is for more teachers of composition in California so that the gifted young people can be taught to compose and conduct. This part of the world is filled with talent but the students haven't the money to go away to school. The greatest thing anyone could do for music would be to bring Ravel, or Hindemith, or perhaps Respighi or Schrecker to teach composition. Schrecker is a fine teacher and he could give us the instruction we need in modern music."

"I don't know anything that Schrecker has written except the *Birthday of the Infanta* which Bruno Walter played for us," I replied to Rodzinski.

"Schrecker has also written operas and some very serious things. Ravel, too, is marvelous. But," continued Rodzinski sternly, "America would rather import compositions. I don't see why they cannot support a large school here, where nature is so beautiful. They need that more than anything."

"Can't compositions be written for the piano and then orchestrated?" I asked.

"Not very well. Some persons do go to the piano and write something down and then orchestrate the piece but it is not very satisfactory. Chopin and Schumann are not good for orchestration because their music is written for the piano. It is a good idea for a composer to play in the orchestra and get the feeling of the music in that way. One has to hear the music orchestrally to accomplish anything worth while."

XXVII

HOWARD HANSON

"IT IS too bad that Mr. Eastman did not live to see his dreams realized. They are being slowly fulfilled but I cannot help wishing that he might be here to watch the development of his plans."

Through his spectacles Howard Hanson watched the swaying of the silver branches on the reed-like eucalyptus trees. Occasionally he turned to look at Al Hendrickson and Newell Armsby, who were stretched upon the bright colored leather cushions by the pool.

Dressed for swimming, the trio luxuriated in a sun bath before a plunge. While he described his musical activities Hanson studied the distorted circles and triangles of light and shade playing over the brown limbs of the bathers.

A toy Pomeranian raced breathlessly over the terrace after a tennis ball. Hanson smiled as Al Hendrickson coaxed the excited puppy away from his game with a small piece of cake.

"Yes," repeated the director from Rochester,

"it is too bad that Mr. Eastman could not have lived to see the working out of his ideas."

"Was Eastman very fond of music? Or were his gifts made from a philanthropic motive?" asked Hendrickson.

"He loved music," answered Hanson quietly, "as much as any man I have ever known. But it was only in later years that he began to like Bach —for he insisted that Bach was written for the organ and he did not care for organ music."

"Eastman interested himself in the whole Rochester University, did he not?"

"After he had helped the music school he endowed the University. The music school is now a part of the University but originally it was a small institution in Rochester. Mr. Eastman took it over and built it into its present organization. Out of two thousand students attending the University five hundred were enrolled as music students."

The tall, lanky, stooped-shouldered Hanson rose from his lounging chair to throw himself down upon the cushions by his companions. His straight straw-color hair straggled above thin delicately modeled features; the lines of a sensitive mouth were exaggerated by a full, red lower lip. From his slender throat came a voice, full and resonant, humorously falling at times into a nasal Yankee twang.

"Being in California seems like a home-coming to me," he commented. "Although I was born in the Northwest much of my youth was spent here."

"Weren't you at the College of the Pacific?" asked Newell Armsby.

"For a time. I was Dean of Music there; later I went abroad to study."

"And you won the *Prix de Rome*," commented Newell with a look of admiration at the boyish figure near him. "Tell us," urged Newell, "something about your *Romantic* Symphony. We are to hear it, are we not?"

"Yes, at my concert. What can I tell you about it?" Hanson reflected. "I wrote the work to commemorate the Boston Symphony's fiftieth anniversary."

"And you have an opera coming out at the Metropolitan this fall, I hear, with Larry Tibbett singing the lead." Al Hendrickson spoke as he was putting the little Pomeranian down upon the lawn for another romp with the tennis ball.

"Yes, I have just finished a concert performance of the opera in Chicago. I conducted and John

Charles Thomas sang the lead. There was only one week for drilling the orchestra. The work we had to do, in so short a time, was terrific."

"What is the style of the opera?" asked Newell.

"*Merry Mount* is melodious. I believe in melody," Hanson remarked seriously. "Think of the Italians! They go out for music; they are not even concerned with the exterior of their singers. I also believe that if opera could be given in English with cultivated diction it would have more success than it now has in America. Some of those who patronize opera assert that they do not care what the characters on the stage are supposed to say; but that is not the right sentiment. A composer works very hard to have his music convey the idea of the text and to make his accompaniment unite with the words. The story should be heard if only to better appreciate the music. Foreign operas should be translated by someone who is able to keep the poetic content. I heard *Don Giovanni* given in English. I do not recall the name of the translator, but it is a perfect work and must have been a labor of love."

"Do you find much real talent among your students?" Hanson was asked.

"Yes, there is talent, but my desire is to make

good teachers rather than to hunt for genius.
Genius declares itself." Continuing to explain his
ideas Hanson spoke of modern schemes for writing music. "I do not think that some of the composers in the field to-day are of the first rank. The
methods they employ are often not sincere. People do not really feel or think in polytonality or
atonality. I can't make out what men are doing
when they write things which are nothing but un-
related notes or intervals mirroring each other. I
don't know what it all means except that they are
striving for something. They cannot feel that way
or think that way. I remember a piece by a composer standing at the top of one of the groups of
modernists. He brought me a work of his. There
wasn't a major triad in it and I said to him: 'Why
haven't you used a major triad? Did you avoid it
on purpose or did you feel that you didn't need
it?' he answered me quite boldly to the effect that
he had never felt the need of it. My reply was:
'You could not have written a piece and never
thought of the major triad.' 'Yes,' he insisted, 'I
did not even notice, up to now, that I had not
used it.' "

Hanson's brows puckered with disgust. He
threw a lump of sugar from the low tea table over

to the puppy and finished his little description of
the objectionable modernist:

"When that man declared he didn't know that
he had not used a major triad it was too much for
me. I turned on him sharply and said:

" 'Look here! Don't try to make me believe that
for it won't go.'

"A funny thing took place later apropos of what
I have been telling you," Hanson laughed. "This
very same man who ignored major triads later
heard Toscanini conduct the *Romantic* Symphony
and came to me in great excitement, almost shouting that he too was 'going romantic' and assur-
ing me that I had the right idea. Isn't that an absurd way of looking at work, as if anyone could
say he is going to be a thing and just be it! Results
don't arrive that way."

"When did Toscanini conduct your symphony?"
asked Al Hendrickson.

"At the beginning of the winter season, and *how*
that New York Philharmonic Orchestra played!
It was superb."

"Do you feel," Hendrickson asked, "that the
Philharmonic plays better for Toscanini than for
other leaders?"

"The results achieved by him are remarkable," declared Hanson, "and for a good reason. Toscanini hears every mistake. If a member of the orchestra plays any note except that one which is before him, or if he plays notes differently from the way in which they are written, Toscanini calls attention to the error immediately. He will ask a horn to go back four bars and repeat the measures. This is done in order that Toscanini may call attention to some fault in interpretation. For example, Toscanini discovered an error in the printed score of the *Romantic*. He said to me, 'You have a certain marking in your manuscript, but in the printed score another indication is given. Which shall I use?' As a matter of fact I had never noticed the difference."

Smiling broadly in appreciation of the incident, Hanson rose slowly from the coral-colored mat upon which he had been lounging. He stepped to the rim of the pool; balanced for a moment before his dive, the leader turned his head to speak again:

"It is said that America has no ideas because she has no folk-songs. It is an absurd statement. We have a greater supply of material than Brahms had when he wrote his great works. For our tunes we may turn to the wonderful songs from the Appalachian Mountains; also to Vermont and to the Elizabethan music of Virginia."

A splash in the blue water ended the discussion.

The next view of Hanson disclosed his long arms reaching out in curving strokes through the ripples as he made his way to the bronze steps on the north side of the pool.

Evening found our guest seated at the piano. A shaft of light fell upon his blond hair. As he played, the composer indulged in a monologue.

"Listen," he exclaimed, "to these modal things. Music of this kind is at least better that the material that has no logic in it; but" he commented as he changed to an old choral, "you cannot improve on this; it is direct; it is beautiful."

"How do you create a work?"

"An idea comes to me. It stirs around in my mind for a year or two before I know just where I am going to use it. For instance, in the *Romantic* I wrote the sub-theme first—you remember it goes like this." Hanson played a melody. "Later I wrote the main theme. The main theme cannot be too melodic as it must be something that can be picked up and used at any time. I like to get a main theme that I can use throughout a symphony."

"Do you know," asked a listener, "in what form you will use your ideas when you have found them?"

"Yes, I really know that by their quality."

"What are you playing now?"

"A poem of Walt Whitman's called *Beat! Beat! Drums!*. I wrote it for one voice but it is too big and I plan to make it into a choral. Would you like to hear something from my opera? Listen! Here are the Pilgrims chanting. The opera opens with this chorus which is heard as the curtain rises. Later the Cavaliers appear. They are described by a very merry, skittish piece of music which contrasts well with the sombre chanting of the Pilgrims. But you must hear the entire opera to really be able to decide whether or not you like it."

"Tibbett will be splendid for your leading rôle."

"None better. I am fortunate also in having Serafin as leader. There will have to be cuts made in *Merry Mount* particularly in the first act. These are necessary in order to tie together certain dramatic situations. And now for my latest."

"What! A new one?"

"Yes, something that has just come to me. It is a pastoral for your theatre. This theme came to me last night; there will be birds and trees, and all that sort of thing. I have a tuneful second theme going already. We are to start," explained Hanson, "somewhat wistfully; then there will be a quick warbling from the flute. Can't you just see the wood scene with the flute imitating the birds? Woodland Theatre is beautiful. I want to put it to music."

XXVIII

OLIN DOWNES

"I DON'T know what is the matter with me. I feel all in and I can't collect my thoughts." Speaking with a trace of self-pity Olin Downes thrust savagely at the grass with his tennis racket as he voiced his disturbed state to the Gunnar Johansens and myself while we were picnicking under the big umbrella-shaped willow trees whose feathery branches swept the cheerful little patch of blue water in our swimming-pool.

I listened without comment to the sigh that followed the complaint but I thought the explanation for that sigh a very simple one and cautiously I spoke to the back of Olin's head which was buried face downward in the cool turf.

"Let me see your engagement book," I suggested.

"I don't want you to see it," Olin grumbled. "It's a disgrace, but here it is; you might as well look at it." Out of a coat pocket came the dog-eared little leather book that was supposed to hold a record of the Downes professional and social dates.

"What's the matter with it, old man?" said Gunnar Johansen soothingly.

"Well, I have only made engagements to eat dinner with three people at the same hour on the same day and I have jotted down luncheons in San Mateo after morning lectures in Carmel which is one hundred miles away; and of course all of these people who have been so kind in asking me to their houses are never going to want to see me again. I need a manager who will follow me around and tell me what to do and when to do it; and then I might be able to keep out of trouble."

"Perhaps you have indigestion, Mr. Downes," politely sympathized young Mrs. Johansen.

"Well, if I haven't it now I deserve to have it, for with all this exercise in the open air I am eating just twice as much as I should."

"You are lecturing at Stanford University this afternoon, are you not?" asked Johansen.

"Yes, I am talking there at four o'clock, which reminds me that I must go in now to the piano and try over some of those passages in the Sibelius First Symphony, for I am going to speak about Sibelius," Olin explained as we strolled up the terrace towards the house.

"Sibelius is perhaps the most lonely and alone of all the composers, for he believes, not from self-consciousness or false pride, but with a real conviction, that he must live a solitary life in order to work at his music and so he stays in Helsingfors where he writes and plans his compositions." Opening the big score, which was lying upon the Steinway, Olin played a few measures.

"All of this music is carefully planned," he observed, "and once Sibelius has his ideas under way he never stops until he has completed his work. He writes for posterity and his music is so elemental in character that it is written for all time. Listen!" Striking a series of rich chords Olin spoke again:

"Here is where the theme stalks in and now here it is again suddenly transformed from its first grim statement into sheer beauty. This bit I am playing to you is just like Sibelius himself— tragic, formidable-appearing, energetic."

"Time to go, sir. You told me to call you at two o'clock," warned William Chambers, the English butler, who is the indefatigable friend and counselor of artists.

"Let me see, William. Is my brown bag in the car? And did you put in my typewriter, for I won't be coming back here to stay to-night."

"Everything is in, sir. You will find your dinner jacket in the top partition of your suitcase if you happen to be needing it to-night."

"What a comfort that man is! And do you know I have a feeling that he really likes me."

Smilingly I followed Olin and the Johansens to the motor and as I stepped through the door I was thinking of the diplomatic William. How many times had I heard Gabrilowitsch, Molinari, and others say:

"What a treasure that man is! And really he seems to like to do things for me."

As we stepped on to the flagging of the driveway William's Saxon blond head bent slightly to Olin in a respectful salute.

"Good-bye and thanks ever so much," called out Olin.

"Good day, sir," answered William's finely modulated tones.

Olin Downes' talks from the platform are enjoyed with the same kind of delight that we experience when a friend confides in us interesting and exciting bits of news. In his search for material during many years of writing Downes has gathered not only the necessary facts about the great per-

sons in music but he has chosen to associate with
the facts the romantic side of his subjects, whose
habits of thought he describes so vividly that we
can actually see their personalities through the
Downes lens.

For example, we are aware of the harshness
of the land about the rugged giant of Helsingfors, or we are made to feel in his music the
deep pounding of the North Sea, whose incessant
monotone leads Sibelius into themes that would
never engage the imagination of an Elgar or
a Respighi. Upon a rushing dynamic torrent of
words we press with Olin Downes, through the
external surroundings that influence the thought
of contemporary writers, on into their inner-
most dreams. With Downes we see the goals
these men have set for themselves upon dizzy
heights which were only attainable by a Beethoven, a Brahms, or a Wagner. In awe we watch
the daring spirits appear climbing the peaks that
never tempt mediocrity. In contrast to the gran-
deur of those artists who use the heroic plan
Downes points to the sparkle of the Spaniards: de
Falla, Albeniz, Granados, whose sunny colors and
deep-toned bells work sorcery upon an audience.

XXIX

FREDERICK STOCK

FREDERICK STOCK brought a crisp note into our rehearsals when, with his precise stroke, he signaled for the opening bars of the Tschaikovsky Fourth Symphony. The orchestra, always on tension under new leadership, hurried along at a strained pace and the effects obtained by this scurrying were pathetically incoherent. Stock, feeling the nervousness in the plunging attacks of the brasses and the oddly halting notes of the woodwinds, concluded that something must be done to establish confidence and checked the music, ordering next the playing of the pizzicato section in which every note was implanted within the memory and upon the finger tips of each player. As the quick phrases leaped from the strings, curving out into a rainbow of tone color through the thick heavy atmosphere of the rehearsal hall, Stock dropped his stick and stood, with folded arms, while he listened gravely to the performance of the orchestra. At the close of the section he commented approvingly:

"I see that you know that piece."

Through the orchestra swept a gust of cheerful laughter as they warmed to the compliment from the leader.

"Now for the Moussorgsky," directed Stock.

Thrum went the strings in their humorous character part in Moussorgsky's *Ballet of the Chickens in the Shells* and from the piccolo shrilled the first cry of the chicks as they burst their shells. Stock, with his coat slung loosely over his shoulders, and with a sparkle in his blue eyes, discoursed during the short intermission upon the Moussorgsky ballet music while he pointed out the appealingly funny incidents in nature contained in the score.

The orchestra gathered about their conductor as he relaxed for a few moments and talked of the Russian school of composers.

A tall and serious-looking young student addressed Stock:

"Moussorgsky's genius is given a place by musicians which sets him above Stravinsky and all who learned from him, is that not true, Mr. Stock?"

"Well, certainly he was the first to bring the ironic humorous note into music which later was given free play by his followers."

"Everyone helped themselves to Moussorgsky's

ideas," said Ernest Bacon looking up from a manuscript that he had been reading and penciling, "and they could do it easily because most of the time he was too befuddled by drink to care what happened to his precious material."

"Yes," Stock agreed, "we hear Moussorgsky scattered through the scores of those who came after him and who were quick to see his talent and to take advantage of the easy opportunity to appropriate his riches."

"This ballet is a good number for these times of depression and it is well to keep many light numbers on our programs," Stock advised, thoughtfully adding: "Music of a lighter character is more suited to the mood of the public and less tiring to minds already weary with anxiety. I shall follow your lead here in keeping away from too profound music even in winter concerts during our next season in Chicago."

"What is going to happen to music in Chicago, Mr. Stock?" questioned Ernest Bacon. "Everything seems to be at sixes and sevens in your city."

"I wish I could answer your question," replied Stock. "If only Mrs. Elizabeth Sprague Coolidge could have remained in Chicago I am sure that she would have done much for us. Now with Mrs.

Edith Rockefeller McCormick gone we are sadly in need of someone who is seriously interested in the survival of symphony and opera. We have only plans for one year more of symphony," continued Stock, "and after that I cannot see anything on the horizon that will assist us with our financial burdens."

Referring to the generosity of our civic leaders in making appropriations for the welfare and maintenance of music in California, Stock commented: "It is the most helpful plan I have heard of and the time will come when cities everywhere will have to help support opera and symphony if we are to have these expensive forms of art."

"Isn't it a pleasure to watch Stock conduct?" remarked Olin Downes enthusiastically as the rehearsal was once again under way. "He is so sure of himself." In further praise of the Chicago leader Downes whispered, "And that is the mark of an experienced director. The inexperienced man is always fussing with the orchestra and has a gesture for everything; but Stock almost believes in a leaderless orchestra. He knows that the men know what to do. It does my heart good to see it."

XXX

CELEBRITIES EXCHANGE IDEAS

"I never could understand how Berlioz failed to reach greater things in music than the works he has given us for orchestra," commented Olin Downes.

Stock, Hamilton Harty, Piastro, and Downes were talking informally after Stock's concert in Woodland Theatre. The four celebrities lingering on in one another's company were discussing composers:

"Don't you call *The Damnation of Faust* great music?" asked Harty in some surprise.

"Yes, that is a masterpiece," Downes answered confidently. "If only Berlioz had written that and nothing else."

"I don't agree with you," Harty replied. "Much of his work for orchestra is unusually fine and I can never understand why musicians rate him as they do, for they certainly undervalue his ability. However, taste is an unknown quantity. For illustration, we all know that Toscanini is accorded a supreme place in the field of orchestra. Now what is it that gives him this unique position?"

"I can tell you," interrupted Stock with fervor. "Toscanini studies and works prodigiously and unceasingly. You may think, Harty, that you have gone over your scores and that you know them backward and forward. And I may think so, too. But you and I put together do not work as persistently as Toscanini."

"That is true, and not only does Toscanini slave for his performances but he has retained all of his enthusiasm for the fine works in music," exclaimed Piastro. "And he is so responsive to the special works which are dear to him that he will stop the orchestra while they are playing some phrase to ask: 'Isn't it beautiful? What difference do you make? What difference do I make when something like this is heard?' "

Olin Downes looked earnestly at Piastro for a moment before he replied:

"Yes, that sounds just like him. And yet with all of his zest for his art, and his knowledge of it, he will not talk about it, at least not for publication. I never shall forget an interview that I had with him once on a train going to Boston. I had been told to get some kind of a story from Toscanini, and as I wondered how I was to persuade him to talk I suddenly remembered that he was to give a concert that night in Boston. 'The very thing,' I decided; 'I will board the train and look up the *Maestro*. He cannot very well escape from me while we are racing along over the country.' "

"I would like to have seen Toscanini's face when you showed up. What did he say?" Stock wanted to know.

"Oh! he was so nice about the whole thing that I felt guilty for intruding," Olin said regretfully, "and after a few attempts to get him to talk I gave it up and reassured him that I would not bother him with my presence. 'Never mind,' I said apologetically, 'I am not going to annoy you with any more questions,' and then I went on alone to Boston where I caught the first train back to New York. But I didn't have a line from Toscanini to quote and the material I had thought I would cunningly secure by traveling in close quarters with Toscanini was missing."

"Sibelius, too, is like that," added Olin. "I asked him for an interview on music and I could see that he was very much troubled by my request and, after a little silence, he said: 'Ich kann nicht.' "

"You know why that is, don't you?" exclaimed Harty ironically. "Sibelius doesn't know about music; he is a composer."

"By the way, Stock, that was a fine performance of the *Meistersinger* that you gave to-day," Olin spoke with a warm note of praise in his words.

"The Wagner," Stock replied, and his ruddy face beamed with appreciation. "What a genius that man was! Think of the second act of *Tristan!* When will you ever hear anything like that? Not in a hundred and fifty years, not in five hundred years, will anything ever be written to equal it."

"Nothing ever will be written like it," interrupted Olin. "And yet how plebeian Wagner can be at times! Sibelius says that *Die Meistersinger* is 'ham and eggs.'"

Stock laughed but quickly defended Wagner:

"There you are," he remarked. "That is it because it comes of the people."

"Undoubtedly," replied Olin, "but it is the pure gold of the people."

"Wagner was always protesting against his environment," commented Stock. "In *Rienzi,* and in all of his music, you hear that desire to escape from his surroundings which dominated him."

"There is a story that illustrates what you

mean," Olin said in his quick manner. "When the *Meistersinger* was given its first performance at Bayreuth after the war, in the scene where Hans Sachs comes in and commences to sing, the audience shouted '*Deutschland über Alles.*' "

Stock again exclaimed:

"There you have it! That is just what Wagner was fighting against always."

Sir Hamilton Harty had been silent as Downes, Stock, and Piastro exchanged ideas which they illustrated cleverly with little episodes. But now he spoke suddenly:

"Wagner's music is immoral," he asserted.

Stock answered him almost casually:

"Of course it is, for it is the soul of Lucifer himself writing."

"But," interrupted Olin Downes, "The immorality of Wagner was only part of the man's soul. The *Nibelungen* shows his ethics and points out that in the depths of his nature he was a profoundly sound, ethical creature."

Harty shrugged his shoulders as he listened to Olin's analysis:

"The ages will tell it all," he replied, "and they are cold critics."

XXXI

MISCHA ELMAN PLAYS HOST

"Why does a critic say that an artist plays in tune or out of tune? And what does he mean when he says it?" Mischa Elman asked this question, turning to Olin Downes who was sipping a demi-tasse after a luncheon with the Elmans in their San Mateo home.

Olin grew thoughtful as he prepared to answer while Elman continued to speculate:

"I know," he said, "that I hear an intonation that to me is out of tune and the next morning I read in the newspaper that the artist's playing was in perfect tune. What is it that the critics are speaking about?"

"I think I can tell you," replied Downes in his decided and energetic manner. "The critic is speaking of something in the quality of the tone played. To illustrate—a man wears a necktie of one color and a coat of another. These two articles of his dress have a different color but either they contrast or they blend as part of the costume, and the same is true with two tones; each may be perfectly in tune but when listened to in relation to one another they produce a dissonance."

Mishel Piastro, who was listening in his impassive way, interrupted Olin Downes:

"Yes, but there is another reason for saying a man plays in tune or out of tune, and it is to be found in an imperfect *vibrato*."

"Yes," added Downes, "you are both correct but what I say about the coat and tie is also true acoustically or scientifically. There must be certain overtones which we hear and then we call a man's playing out of tune."

Elman spoke again abruptly:

"Also, Mr. Downes, if a player hears that he is a little bit out of tune and quickly changes his position he is called out of tune; but I think he is in tune."

"He is out of tune first, however," Olin smilingly objected.

"To change the subject," Elman remarked, "what is your feeling about applause? In Germany you know they never applaud between short numbers, as for instance in an A.B.C. group."

"I know," Olin replied, "but that is wrong. People should not have to wait so long to give expression to their feelings. Take for example a symphony which is played straight through. The audience has no chance to respond after the *scherzo,* which is the bright section, but must wait for an *andante,* or solemn movement at the end of the work, when applause is quite out of place."

"That reminds me," Elman said with a merry laugh, "of a visit I made to the city of Hamburg. I always had some misfortune befall me when I played in that town, and on my last trip I thought that my concert was to be played in the evening, but it was scheduled for the afternoon. I took a late train which landed me at the concert hall just as the concert would have been finished if I had played it at the right hour."

"Another time I was rehearsing with S—— and the orchestra. We were to play the Handel concerto and you know that there is a tradition for a violinist to pause after the *allegro,* for at this point there is a long note for the orchestra to hold, but we always stop entirely and use the opportunity to tune up. I called S——'s attention to this and warned him:

" 'When we finish the *allegro* I stop.'

" 'But we play on,' he replied.

" 'No,' I insisted, 'we all stop.'

"S—— stubbornly resisted: 'We play on.'

"I grew angry and shouted to S——:

" 'Look here, if you play on I don't play with you.'

" 'But you will have to play, for you are responsible for your contract,' restorted S——.

" 'Very well, I will play but I will have a piano accompany me.' "

"Good for you, Mischa, old man! S—— couldn't get around that, could he?" Piastro interrupted with a laugh.

"No," said Elman, "he gave up. 'All right! You stop and we will stop, too,' was his final agreement. But on the day of the concert," continued Elman, "as we were well on our way in the concerto I suddenly began to think: 'Will we stop or will we go on?' I tried desperately to catch S——' eye but he was counting away and would not look at me. We got to the note which the orchestra was to hold and all of us stopped playing. Now, according to German tradition, no one must make a sound. But a few hardy souls thought that they would encourage me by clapping. This was too much for the good *'Deutschland über Alles'* people in the audience and they commenced to hiss at those who had applauded. The din and confusion was

terrific and S—— looked long and pointedly at me.
At last he leaned over from his conductor's stand
and whispered despairingly:

" 'Didn't I tell you? You hear them, don't you?
Now will you listen to me the next time? Didn't
I tell you?' "

"What are the happy moments for an artist,
Elman?" asked Downes while the laughter over
the episode in Germany still rippled heartily in
the voices of the Elman guests.

"The happiest moment? Let me think!" mused
Elman. "Yes, I know. It is when one is conscious of
presence of mind and alertness while everything
moves at the right rate of speed, and coördination
with the audience and the orchestra is perfect.
That is the best moment of all."

"I know what you mean," exclaimed Downes
eagerly, "and how dreadful it is if something goes
wrong in the beginning. When one is talking to an
audience a word mispronounced, or a little mistake at the start, and the mind goes floundering
around for half an hour before it is back to a
coherent state. As you say, the right *tempo* governing the whole performance is everything. One
must not be ahead of the moment or behind it in
his thoughts and I agree with you, Elman, that

if a man can achieve this in his work he can have no greater satisfaction."

"Why is Downes so keen on Sibelius?" whispered Piastro as the guests left the dining room for the more intimate atmosphere of the living room with its soft rugs and great couches.

"Because," answered Marjorie French, "he visited Sibelius who received him in such a kindly fashion that it melted all of the callous critic in Downes."

"No, really, that is not the whole truth," interrupted Fried. "There is a great deal of merit in the work of Sibelius, and Downes may be the self-appointed prophet; but that alone would not cause leaders of symphony concerts to include Sibelius in so many of their programs."

"I don't know. The power of the press is enormous and certainly Sibelius owes Downes an eternal debt of gratitude," said Mischa Elman decidedly. Elman had walked over to listen to the discussion on the merits of Finland's genius. He talked on vivaciously to the clique who had become interested in offering their views upon the increasing popularity of Sibelius.

"Do you like Sibelius?" Mischa Elman asked suddenly while he leaned towards Marjorie who

Friends All

Reading from left to right: Henry Hadley, Alfred Hertz, Leonora Wood Armsby, Ossip Gabrilowitsch, Mrs. Gabrilowitsch, Fritz Reiner, Mrs. Reiner.

had been attentive to the chatter about her in an impersonal fashion.

"I imagine that I have heard Olin talk so much about him that I judge Sibelius through Olin, and not with any particular judgment of my own." Marjorie's reply was cautious. "When Olin describes the rugged earth quality in the violin concerto and the ethereal quality of the material in the piano accompaniment I think that I feel all that it is suggested that I should feel."

Elman shrugged his powerful shoulders and spoke curtly:

"I do not think pieces should have to be explained," he said in a cold, toneless voice.

"Nor I," echoed Piastro.

"Music is abstract thought," insisted Elman, "and cannot be described as a picture."

"Oh! I don't know," Marjorie dissented. "Everything carries a picture with it."

"That is all right to picture for oneself," answered Elman gravely as he regarded Marjorie with a far-off look in his keen eyes, "but the picture must not be imposed upon us by anyone outside ourselves."

XXXII

VICKI BAUM AND RICHARD LERT

THE plane from Los Angeles bringing Richard
Lert to San Francisco made a perfect landing before
the spruce-green and white pavilion at Mills Field.
Passengers filed from the airship's low cabin to
stretch limbs stiffened by long restraint. Weary
smiles betokened relief at being anchored.

A man of slim build strode at the head of the line.
From his sharp-featured, pointed face, crowned
with a fringe of reddish gold hair, green-grey eyes,
obliquely set, looked whimsically over the crowd
swarming about the moored craft.

Joe Thompson, John Rothschild and I noted
the distinguished figure. In unison we exclaimed:
"Richard Lert!"

The wind must have blown our words, for a
clear musical voice answered:

"Yes, this is Richard Lert."

"But we expected Mrs. Lert," called back Joe
Thompson.

"Vicki? She is in New York supervising the

preparations for her new play *The Divine Drudge.*
She joins me here on Thursday. My two boys are
motoring north to be with us."

From his corner in the motor that carried us
to San Francisco Lert volunteered information
about his family.

"We came to Hollywood on account of my
wife's plays. They are being filmed. You ask how I
like the movie colony. We have seen but little of
it as we have been in Hollywood only a short time.
It is difficult for us to meet strangers since we
speak very little English." Lert spoke regretfully.
"My boys use English in school but not when they
are at home." A benign fatherly smile played about
Lert's eyes. It vanished as he asked for data con-
nected with his programs:

"I think it was a good idea to choose light
Viennese music since we had so little time for
more serious works. *Rosenkavalier* and *Tales from
Vienna Woods* please an audience. Tell me about
the soloist?"

"Gunnar Johansen? He is excellent. You know
that he is going to play the Brahms Piano Concerto
No. 2."

"I wonder," mused Lert, "if it will be too heavy
for a Sunday afternoon concert."

"Gunnar does not think so," I replied quickly, "since the second half of the program is so gay."

"Perhaps," answered Lert.

*   *   *   *

"Vicki is here!"

Lert's jubilant tone vibrated through the telephone receiver. It was apparent that the protective presence of Mrs. Lert (Vicki Baum) had brightened his outlook. New tasks were less formidable with someone to forestall the petty annoyances and interruptions which harass a leader.

"And she wants to see you. Can you come to tea at the Western Women's Club this afternoon? Vicki is to be guest of honor."

The club was crowded when I stopped there at five o'clock. Reception rooms were flooded with light and awhirl with excitement. "Lookouts" by the elevators watched every up-coming car. The world-celebrated writer stepped unexpectedly out of a narrow bronze cage into the vestibule.

"Vicki Baum!" whispered many lips.

The feverish atmosphere subsided as the author of *Grand Hotel* commenced to speak to the assembly.

"I must ask you to let me greet you in this way.

It would take all of our time if I should attempt to speak to you individually. There could be no exchange of ideas between us."

Vicki Baum's white teeth gleamed through full, red lips as she talked. Her large and expressive grey eyes, under jet-black brows, played over the faces turned raptly upon her. The charm of her presence excited the crowd. They responded in a low hum of admiration.

"Would you like to ask me some questions?" she suggested.

A thin, tired voice struggling against timidity was the first response.

"Where do you get your ideas for a story?"

"From different sources. I see a little house by the roadside. Perhaps it is only a small cottage with a tiny garden. I look at it and wonder what kind of people live in it. Soon I picture characters I think might be like the persons who own the house. I ask myself what they think about—what they do—and what is to happen to them. I go on thinking and thinking sometimes for years about those imaginary beings. One day I see my story and begin to write it."

"It must be great fun," a listener wistfully commented.

"Yes! Great fun," returned Vicki Baum, "but great work, too."

Questions! Questions! They were endless.

"Does it take you long to finish a book?"

"What do you think of American women?"

"Do you mind telling us how you feel about Hitler?"

Vicki Baum's patience was superb. The air was filled with smoke from cigarettes. A hand jerked open one of the tall windows and the draught caught the fragrance of tea simmering in a Russian samovar. Mrs. Edward Dexter Knight, the club's president, led her guest from the platform:

"Come and have some refreshments," she urged. "You have been so generous."

Vicki Baum cast one last radiant smile upon her admirers before she stepped into the throng.

*　　*　　*　　*

On Tuesday morning Vicki Baum and I chatted in the lobby of the Clift Hotel. We waited for Lert who was sending off telegrams.

"Your costume looks very European," I remarked admiringly.

There was that stamp to the white serge suit,

with its black satin scarf and black beret, that said "Vienna."

"Do you like it? I have a suit much like the one you are wearing. I like these plain things."

"But your coat has the military shoulders. They are very smart."

"I had a time getting my tailor to put them in. I have a Viennese tailor in New York who makes my suits. When I said: 'You must put square shoulders in my jacket,' he objected with 'But they are not good-looking and they are not dignified.'"

"What has become of your boys?" I asked after a glance at the clock above the newsstand.

"They are getting their swimming suits and the 'old man' Lert is over there writing a telegram to Alfred Hertz. Hertz asked Richard to a rehearsal of the Standard Oil program but he could not find the hall. Here they come! Now we can get started."

As we headed for Burlingame Vicki Baum looked fondly at Lert and her two sons. Her yellow, bobbed hair glistened under the black satin beret. Lert held himself proudly like the triumphant captain of a winning team. The ways of this family were endearing through naturalness and frankness.

"I am a musician, too," confided Mrs. Lert. "I played the harp with many of the symphony orchestras of Europe."

"How did you become a writer?"

Lert answered for his wife:

"She was always writing sketches and stories. We were surprised, however, when *Grand Hotel* made a success in America, as in Europe it had no such fame."

Vicki Baum interrupted Lert: "I never felt *Grand Hotel* to be one of my best books," she confided. "The book that I like the best is one that has not become popular. I feel sorry about this as I would over an unsuccessful child."

"Everyone says your new book *As Life Goes On* is excellent."

"Thanks! I like to hear it; but if Sinclair Lewis had said it I would be very pleased."

"Tell us something about Sinclair Lewis," I coaxed. "What is he like?"

"Very simple—very kind—very good-natured. The first time I saw Lewis was just as I docked at New York. My publisher had sent for me to come over. It was early morning and I did not expect to be met. A very long man walked towards me. At his side was another very long man. The first man introduced himself as 'Doubleday,' my publisher. 'And I have brought along an interpreter," he explained as he glanced at the man with him. 'I don't speak German, so I thought I might need someone to help me out.'

" 'What can we do for you?' asked the interpreter.

" 'Just explain to the inspector that the bottles in my dressing-case do not contain anything alcoholic. They are only toilet water.'

"Doubleday pointed out the tall buildings on the sky-line. Suddenly he began to laugh. 'I can't keep the secret any longer,' was his explanation. 'That man I introduced as my interpreter is Sinclair Lewis.' Wasn't it dear of them to come down to welcome me? We left the boat together and went off to eat breakfast."

Lert, who was looking quietly into his wife's grey eyes, spoke gently:

"So many people you have to meet in your work; so many letters to write; so much to do; it keeps you busy all the time."

"Yes," replied Vicki Baum wistfully, "I am working, working, working; with no time for my family, no time for fun."

One of the young Lerts looked at his mother.

He called her attention to the road: "I thought we came into San Francisco from the other side of the city. Is this the way to Burlingame?"

"Yes," she answered, "see the trees; we are getting into the country."

I asked Vicki Baum if she were going to write while she was on her visit to Northern California.

"Not on this visit. No! I want to rest."

"But you will," said Lert, "I know. One day you will be at it and that will be the last of you until the book is finished."

"I *am* working on a book now, but I have put it aside." Vicki Baum brushed the hair back from the youngest son's forehead while she murmured: "I want to be with them."

"Does it take you long to finish a novel?"

"Yes," was the answer, "but my best work I wrote in three weeks. I always feel sorry for myself when I write; I say to myself: 'Poor thing, shut up away from your family and from all pleasures'; but I have to do it so I just go away by myself until it is over."

"This is fine!" Lert exclaimed as the motor put us down at my place.

We hurried into the garden.

Vicki Baum pulled off her beret and took a

deep breath that brightened her cheeks with color. "The boys," she said, "must get right into their swimming suits."

On the lawn were friends who had come to see the Lerts.

"I would rather be the author of *Grand Hotel* than anyone else on earth," exclaimed a woman.

"I have another book I like even better," was the reply.

Relaxing in a wicker chair under the willows Vicki Baum enjoyed very much her favorite rôle, that of being Mrs. Lert and the mother of the young Lerts. I wondered as I watched her simplicity if she were not surprised to find how much she counted for in the great world. I listened as a woman spoke of the sentiment in the nature of the German people. To illustrate her thought she continued:

"Often in one of the forests in Germany you see a girl walking with a young man. The couple have just been married. He is dressed in woolen clothes and she wears a skirt and blouse made from the material which is left over from his suit."

"I know," said Vicki Baum eagerly. "In her short skirt and thick stockings she walks at his side. They hold hands. Could anything," asked the au-

thor of *Grand Hotel,* "be more beautiful than to
walk with the man you love while you hold his
hand? This is real love; not love because it is con-
venient for the man or woman to find security in
one another, or in money. Such a love comes only
in youth. It is the perfect thing—the perfect experience. Besides this nothing else is of real value."

Silence fell upon the company for an instant.
Many thoughts traveled to cherished memories,
led there by Vicki Baum's description of a first
romance.

"You don't mind my saying that I was surprised
when I saw you. My idea of you was quite different."

The exclamation from a listener made Vicki
Baum laugh heartily.

"What had you in mind about me?"

"I thought you would be older and a brunette."

"You are right, my dear. I am older and I am a
brunette."

"I suppose you are continually dogged by inter-
viewers," continued the curious one.

"Much of the time; and I am still not used to it.
Since I came to San Francisco I am constantly surrounded by reporters and people who want me to
speak over the radio, or to attend receptions."

"But you are a celebrated person; you must not forget that."

"Sometimes I do forget it," was the modest answer, "for I do not take my books too seriously. Perhaps I should not say that. I am in earnest about my work, but my husband and my boys come first. They are the really important part of my life. My writings are my fun. What do you think of my husband's conducting?"

"We like it so much," the group about the celebrity answered in chorus.

"Richard was disappointed that he could not lead a symphony so that he might show what he can do with the serious compositions."

"But we loved his Viennese things. We do not have enough of this kind of music."

Vicki Baum smiled happily: "Richard is a dear," she said fervently. "I travel about a great deal and I meet many men but none that I think as fine as my man."

XXXIII

CONCERNING DESTINIES

LAWRENCE TIBBETT parked his electric-blue roadster in the shadows of two massive oaks.

"I took the short cut and got lost," he explained gaily. "I never can remember the right twists and turns of these back roads. Is Jane here?"

"She is having tea in the garden with the Gabrilowitsches."

Tibbett beamed contentedly as he exclaimed:

"I thought I would find her here. Are there many people at the pool?"

"Gabrilowitsch and his daughter are swimming. The Alfred Hendricksons are with Jane."

We crossed the terrace. The man at my side walked unhurriedly through the dew cooled grass. I looked at his coatless figure wearing a snug-fitting canary-yellow sweater, grey flannel trousers, and while canvas shoes. Evidently exercise was part of the day's program.

Scenes and episodes from Tibbett's life crowded into my mind. There was Bakersfield! In this inland California town Larry Tibbett acquired his intrepid courage while his shoulders gained sturdiness. Tibbett's occupation in Bakersfield was farming. Forced to fling his strength against the obstinate earth while his plow dug through broad fields he amused himself by singing. The slow pace of the plow was accompanied by sentimental ballads or songs of heroic adventures.

At times the urge of a career stirred Tibbett and beckoned him away from the peaceful valley tranquilly sunning its long expanse below the mountains. As he strode through belts of ripening grain the man who whistled and sang developed a force that exerted itself not only through his muscular frame with its full throat and erect head but poured out its giant strength into aspirations for fame through the medium of his voice. Tibbett knew that he could not be financially safeguarded should failure overwhelm him; nevertheless he pressed on with his artistic ambitions.

When we remember how this artist was molded for his destiny it is not strange that we find him responsive to the ordinary feelings of simple people. An understanding of human needs is Larry Tibbett's richest possession. It accounts in large measure for the grip that he holds over countless thousands of admirers. It is the warm beating of a heart once strained earthward that appeals to us when we listen to Tibbett intoning "That's Why Darkies Were Born." Perhaps it is a memory of rose vines in country gardens that brings a languid pensiveness into the verses he so softly sings to "Sylvia."

*   *   *   *

"Tea?" suggested Leonora Hendrickson as the singer joined the group about the tea table.

"Not just now, thanks," was the reply. "Hello there! Is that Gabrilowitsch?"

A head floating on the water looked up and acknowledged the greeting.

"How is the water?" returned Tibbett.

"Perfect," pronounced Gabrilowitsch from a halo of ripples.

"I'm coming in. I'll be with you in a jiffy." Tibbett disappeared through the evergreen arch that leads to the orchard and the bath-houses.

"Larry is busy with Hanson's opera *Merry Mount*," confided Jane Tibbett. "He is working hard and needs exercise but I wish he would swim before three o'clock."

"You are afraid it is too cold?" asked Leonora

Hendrickson. Reassuringly she added: "Larry will have time for a sun bath and he can take hot tea or sherry to warm him."

"What does your husband think of Hanson's *Merry Mount?*"

At Clara Gabrilowitsch's question Jane Tibbett who was embroidering a square of tapestry stopped her sewing and paused. She listened attentively before responding:

"He likes it. There are superb chorals and beautiful melodies in the score. Larry throws himself so intensely into every part he portrays and the rôle of Bradford, which he plays in *Merry Mount* calls for vigorous acting. Larry has been singing at the Bohemian Grove."

Leonora Hendrickson interrupted at this point to say:

"I hear the whole entertainment was marvelous. Gabrilowitsch they tell me, played divinely; John Charles Thomas sang beautifully and Larry was at his best." With eyes that sparkled admiration Leonora watched the two celebrities who were revolving around one another in the water.

Tibbett suddenly decided that he had finished his swim. He swung himself over the side of the pool to lie upon the grass.

"You were talking about the concert at the grove," he said. "I wondered how Gabrilowitsch could play in that chilly air."

"Was it so cold?" queried Clara Gabrilowitsch.

"I know," Tibbett declared, "that I stood up to sing a tone and I wondered how it was going to sound. I could see it mirrored in a thick white mist and it wavered as it cut through the air."

Jane Tibbett shivered. "Have some tea," she counseled.

"I hear that you are studying *Merry Mount*," I remarked to Tibbett. "Hanson played us parts of the score when he was here."

"You must come over some morning when I practise."

"It doesn't disturb you to have listeners?"

"On the contrary. I like to know what people are thinking. The artist is only one part of an equation—the other part is a human soul like you or me. A listener must be made to feel that what he hears coincides with his own idea of the emotion that the composer has written about. The story of *Merry Mount* grips me. It is magnificent and the text excellently handled. When I am reading the libretto I am thrilled through and through. However, Hanson may have to make some cuts."

"Composers do get carried away with their ideas," commented one of the coterie.

Operas and their composers were dismissed from the conversation as Tibbett's gaze traveled to Gabrilowitsch.

"I like Gabrilowitsch so much," the singer said in a low voice to his neighbor.

"Yes, he has a rich personality," she murmured.

"He has something more—a kindness and a loving quality in his nature. I feel that even upon my slight acquaintance with him."

Tibbett wanted to know whether Gabrilowitsch had ever been attracted by any career other than music.

"He is the best person to answer your question," replied Clara. "Ossip, come and join us," she coaxed.

The Director drew near.

"We were wondering," Tibbett exclaimed, "how you decided to become an orchestra leader."

"Oh, I suppose every little boy has some idea of what he wants to be when he grows up—a policeman, a fireman, or a soldier—something valiant. I wanted to conduct."

"Did your parents object?"

"No, my father, who was a lawyer, was very fond of music. I have a brother who is not a professional musician, but he plays the violin and also the piano exceptionally well."

"And your father-in-law, Mark Twain, liked music, I understand. I so often wonder what it must be like to write as he did. Was his literary work difficult for him?"

Clara Gabrilowitsch answered Tibbett:

"My father found writing laborious at times. He planned his stories while walking up and down the floor of his study. Sometimes he wrote them just as they came to his mind but often he worked hard over them. My father," Clara explained, "was serious and profound under his vein of humor. He has been wrongly described as moody. He was never that but he saw life clearly."

"Many literary men are interested in music and some are excellent critics," declared Ossip.

"Yes, Romain Rolland is a good example," observed Jane Tibbett. "His *Jean Christophe* is wonderful and his *Beethoven* very fine."

"Apropos of Rolland," said Gabrilowitsch, "I have a little story which may amuse you. I was about ten years old. I was staying with my father in a European hotel. One afternoon I was playing the piano. As I finished my 'impromptu recital' a piece of paper was handed to me. On it was written: 'I am leaving now without having had a chance to speak to you but I heard you playing and I predict that some day you will be a great pianist.' The note was signed 'Romain Rolland.' The name did not signify anything to me at that time. Some years later I was living in a European town. Close to us was Rolland's home. My sister who always kept family souvenirs produced the note he had sent me. Rolland," declared Gabrilo-witsch with an amused smile crinkling the corners of his pensive mouth, "could not remember the occasion at all."

"But," continued the pianist, "to return to my career. I was fortunate to have been allowed to do the work I wanted to do. Think of men who have been thrown by fate into occupations for which they have no taste and for which they are un-suited."

"There is Kerensky," one of our group ex-claimed, "forced out of Russia. I am told that he is now writing for a newspaper in Paris."

"I can think of a number of men who have shown complete disintegration of their personal-ties through a change of occupation," observed Gabrilowitsch. "I have watched great natures literally shrink into themselves when forced into rôles that are distasteful. Mussolini is an example of a leader who has remained in the position where he can best express himself. And you"— Gabrilowitsch turned to Tibbett— "must feel that you have found the right medium."

"Strangely enough," Larry replied, "I wanted to be a conductor. I chose singing for my career because it was necessary for me to gain a livelihood."

"Have you a philosophy which helps you to solve your problem?" asked Gabrilowitsch.

"I believe that nothing is ever lost," was the answer.

"That is Hegel's philosophy," declared Ossip.

Tibbett continued:

"I do not like to think of the past. It seems a waste of time to dwell on something which cannot be changed. The present and the future are different."

"If," asked Gabrilowitsch, "you think the present and the future can be changed how do you account for the fact that some people spend their lives in an environment which keeps them from achieving the things they are capable of?"

"Perhaps," said Larry thoughtfully, "they fail to see new situations as fresh opportunities. After all, although Kerensky was forced out of Russia he was given his chance to prove himself through the downfall of the Empire. Speaking of Russia, that was a lovely Fugue for Violins and Violas by Dubensky that you played to-day."

"Wasn't it?" agreed Clara enthusiastically. "It is a joy to hear a modernist who can keep away from all the discords that we are 'treated to' by our contemporary composers."

"Yes," Larry agreed, "the modernists give us much that is unpleasant; however, I have just found some songs that have been set to good music. The composer has quite frankly said to himself: 'I am going to put Shakespeare's verse to music that I feel is appropriate for the words. This music shall be what I think myself. It must be independent of what other composers feel to be the proper setting for Shakespeare's words.' There is a song on Hamlet's soliloquy—bits of *King Lear*. There are dozens of them and they are glorious."

"Do you mind telling me how you learn your songs?" asked Clara.

"I get a song or an opera through studying out,

not so much with the ear although the ear is necessary at times. I really pick up the music with
my larynx or throat muscles, for I study the impressions made upon them."

"And your programs? How do you choose their
material?"

"A program should have in its make-up something for each listener. When I sing I hate to have
anyone go away and say: 'What a poor concert!
There wasn't a thing on the program I cared
for.'"

"Yes," Gabrilowitsch affirmed with earnestness,
"people must be permitted to enjoy the music
which pleases them. If the public is to be attracted
to concerts compositions must be performed that
have interest for the majority of music lovers."

XXXIV

DISTINGUISHED GUESTS: RUSSIAN MUSIC

AT A concert in the Hollywood Bowl, sponsored by Mr. and Mrs. Edward Doheny of Los Angles, Gabrilowitsch played the Tschaikovsky Concerto No. 1 with the Los Angeles Symphony Orchestra accompanying him.

Gabrilowitsch was to play during the second part of the program and while he was waiting for his number he sat in the conductor's box with his wife, his daughter, and one or two guests. When it was time for him to appear upon the stage he slipped out of his chair and after requesting us to call for him after the concert he left us remarking somewhat regretfully:

"Good-bye! Here is where I go to work."

In a short time the big concert piano was shoved before the footlights. The orchestra seated themselves; then looked about the amphitheatre a bit consciously. Gabrilowitsch stepped out from the shadowed back-curve of the great shell to take his place at the piano. The *forte* passages in the opening movement of the concerto zoomed through the midsummer night.

As I listened, a desire seized me to present the same program at Woodland Theatre. Just a year later Celia Tobin Clark sponsored a concert for the Philharmonic at which Gabrilowitsch was heard in his rôle of both conductor and pianist. He gave us the Tschaikovsky. Many who heard the beautiful concerto on this occasion must think often and gratefully of Celia Clark, whose assistance enabled us to offer this fine program to our friends.

On the day of the memorable performance I drove Ossip and Clara Gabrilowitsch to the theatre after an early luncheon at my house. My hands were cold with excitement but I tried to keep up a natural conversation with Gabrilowitsch. Our motor passed through the twisting country lanes bordered by yellow blossoming acacia trees. As we neared San Mateo we came upon the first cars parked by the roadside—left by owners attending the concert. Soon we could count hundreds and hundreds of cars which were interspersed by bulky Greyhound buses.

On the footpaths lines of people dressed in light,

gay country clothes were making their way to the concert grounds.

"Isn't it wonderful to see them?" I asked Gabrilowitsch who laughed at my enthusiasm.

"You had better wait until you see if the theatre is filled before you die of happiness!" he teasingly suggested, but his merry eyes had become grave as he watched the crowd hurrying by.

Our car stopped before the conductor's little house. The door was swung open by Frank Mason, the reliable chauffeur, who has driven dozens of conductors back and forth from San Francisco to the theatre without a mishap or a slip in punctuality. Walter Oesterreicher greeted me and took Gabrilowitsch's briefcase from his hand. We walked into the tiny rest-house built solely for the use of our leaders. Its green roof and painted window-boxes, filled with pink geraniums, cast a ray of cheerfulness upon the parched brown grass that straggled over the dusty field back of the stage. Within, everything had been arranged by Mrs. Howard Loveland for the comfort of the artist. A carafe of water and a thermos bottle of orange-ade stood on the table near a wicker reclining couch.

"How you spoil your directors!" said Gabrilowitsch lightly but gratefully. On the platform
back of the stage the orchestra was practising. With
fiddles tucked beneath their chins, or softly blowing on flutes and clarinets, they swept fleetly
through difficult passages as they warmed up for
the overture.

"It is fine weather; the concert should be beautiful," was the comment from the musicians as
with Clara Gabrilowitsch I made my way across
the side passageway of the platform. My guest and
I paused for a moment to look at the scene before us.

Haidee Pohlman, our executive secretary, and
Everett Jones, our publicity agent, stood at
the main entrance speeding the progress of the
throngs.

Episodes from Chaucer's *Canterbury Tales*
crossed my mind as I looked at the many sides of
life represented by the inflowing audience. People of the stage, dignitaries of the various denom-
inations of religion, writers, *débutantes, grand
dames,* polo players, men of finance, were filing
into the seats and boxes. Jane Cowl's lovely dark
beauty dazzled; so did Ina Claire's radiant smile
and there was gentle purpose written on the intel-

ligent thoughtful face of Katharine Cornell. With Noel Sullivan was the picturesque Ramon Navarro. Gertrude Atherton and Kathleen Norris dominated their groups. The powers from the universities were present, Mrs. Herbert Hoover—Dr. and Mrs. Ray Lyman Wilbur and Dr. and Mrs. Warren Allen of Stanford with their friends occupied the Stanford box; Mills College was represented by Dr. Amelia Rinehardt and the Luther Marchants, and Berkeley by Dr. Douglas Campbell. In another corner of the theatre were the Menuhin family, the Mischa Elmans, Ruggiero Ricci, Margery Fischer and the Lawrence Strausses. These and other celebrities made a distinguished and interesting company.

The theatre was filling rapidly. I grew disturbed as to whether or not we could seat all our patrons. What could we do with the overflow audience? There had been an attempt on other occasions when similar conditions faced us to seat our guests in boxes which were not used, but this had brought protest from some of the owners. It was unfortunate that on our big days many visitors had nothing but standing-room although extra chairs had been placed wherever a space could be found for them. The more youthful and enthusiastic music-lovers were beginning to seat themselves along the wall above the ravine and occasionally a very lively youngster perched himself high in the oak boughs joining our feathered friends of the symphony—the bright caroling birds. It was a tribute to the genius of Gabrilowitsch—this surging crowd.

In my box I found Dean John Sellards of Stanford. We stood together for a few moments looking over the thousands of people about us. Much of the enthusiastic support of the theatre had been due to the efforts of Jack Sellards whose ideas for interesting Stanford students had proved invaluable and successful in selling the student books.

"If only the aeroplanes will leave us alone today," I whispered to Raymond Armsby. "We have orders from Washington posted at all the fields, and Crissy and Mills fields usually are very good about flying away from our direction. But I think we may get some of the oil planes or a private plane. Seeing the crowd or hearing the music makes them fly over our heads out of curiosity."

Almost as I spoke a huge grey aeroplane came circling towards us. The hum of the motor in the still spaces turned into a terrific roar as the machine sailed straight over the theatre. Is there any more helpless feeling than to be sitting under one of those serene ships of the sky and to be deafened and drowned by its noise without being able to utter a protest?

"Well," said Jack Sellards soothingly, "perhaps that is the end of the miserable pests for the day."

My anxiety disappeared as the orchestra walked out upon the stage. First violins to the left, 'cellos to the right with Piastro and Penha alert and ready for the opening bars. A hush fell upon the crowd which awaited Gabrilowitsch's arrival upon the platform.

The Detroit leader appeared wearing his spotless white and what he called his "Hillsborough soft collar." Always a magnetic personality, on this day his great gifts lifted Gabrilowitsch to lofty heights.

The orchestra also had taken on a more important look as it was augmented for Stravinsky's suite *The Fire Bird*. To the left of the stage the concert-grand piano was especially noticeable through its proximity to the swan-like harps whose glitter always adds poetry and romance to the sombre coloring in the orchestra. Kajetan Attl, our harpist, was placing the proud-looking curved instruments in line. Our harps stand out clearly, for the tall, dark, jade-green cypresses just behind them throw their brows into high relief. It is always heart-touching when Attl with his skill for making his instrument sing, plucks out the beautiful *arpeggios*. The familiar faces of Eugene Hayes, in charge of the second violins, and Vladimir Drucker, one of the finest trumpeters in America, were tense with expectation while Otto Kegel, our librarian and also a trumpeter, gazed from the corner of his eye at the music racks so carefully prepared by him hours before the performance.

On Gabrilowitsch's program the Tschaikovsky B flat minor concerto replaced the symphony. The concert offered an all-Russian program starting with Glinka's overture to *Russlan and Ludmila*. Then came Gliere's *The Sirens*. From these exponents of Russian genius we whirled into the gorgeous, exotic suite from the ballet of *The Fire Bird*.

How Stravinsky manages to stimulate us as he does is one of those questions that puzzle us as we are drawn by his imagination through a world which is both real and unreal. His magic is really very white magic when one has become accustomed to the wealth of suggestion used by the composer. *The Fire Bird* is a work with appeal.

The music describes the weird figures of the ballet and always suggests that it is fantasy not life of which Stravinsky is writing.

Intermission time interrupted our Russian feast and the audience strolled out into the parade ground for orangeade and conversation. From the back section of the fan-shaped amphitheatre there is a perfect view of the entire enclosure. It is a delight to watch the leaves fall quietly from the oaks upon the stone floor and the curve of the hills beyond—rising like details in a drop-curtain.

The big grand piano was wheeled out to the centre of the stage and an instant later the orchestra, under the direction of Piastro, assembled a little to the rear of the platform. Gabrilowitsch seated himself at the piano and, after a rapid survey of the rapt faces in the theatre, the opening bars of the concerto were driven out like arrows flying from a giant bow. Deftly the music was made to spin under the sure and steady hands of Gabrilowitsch. We listened to the passionate outburst from the dark and disillusioned soul of Tschaikovsky softened by moods of gentle pathos and acceptance of the pain of life.

Nature, as if in touch with the composer's moods, threaded the skies with little strands of fog from great cloud banks. These began to drift in small streamers close to us. The air chilled. In a final surging of supreme expression the last phrases of the concerto moved towards us. Gabrilowitsch raised his head which had been bent over the piano, his hands resting motionless a moment upon the keys. It was still in the theatre—very still. Our thoughts crept back from the sublime abstract to the dear, common things of earth. A little boy jumped down from his perch in the oaks and his feet, clattering on the stones, seemed to awaken us to a realization of what was happening. Now Gabrilowitsch rose from the piano and the applause broke and crashed through the theatre, pouring itself forth to die against the painted walls.

A great artist stepping forth from his superior world into our little affairs is always a bit terrifying, and we almost shrink from contact with him for we feel unequal in the meeting, and our attempts to be sociable seem hopelessly futile. But as I led the Gabrilowitsches through a jam of friends and admirers, awaiting them at the George Camerons after the concert, I felt that the constraint so often paralyzing on such an occasion was lacking, and we pressed forward through the

crowded rooms out to the wide verandah where
Helen Cameron was busy with her guests. I saw
everywhere admiration in the eyes which were
trained upon Gabrilowitsch and soon he was the
centre of a circle of lovely creatures who gave him
cakes and tea and homage. A greatly astonished
male guest strolled up to me and remarked:

"I've just been talking to your conductor; he's
a regular fellow, isn't he?"

"You are right; he is," I replied.

Music had been driven from our midst by the
advent of late autumn weather, school opening in
the little, low, tile Spanish buildings adjacent to
our theatre, and the fact that our orchestra would
soon be rehearsing for the San Francisco opera
season, which, when opened, would attract the
musical public to the ravishment offered by divas,
"golden-voiced" tenors and snowy white tulle ballet skirts. The wind frisked now through the uncovered Woodland Theatre, and the box tiers,
emptied of their gay orange cords, and the emer-
ald green chairs had the look of a fan from which
the decorated covering had been torn, exposing
its bare ribs to the pity of those who had loved its
former brilliance.

But it was good to be free from the cares of

budgets and deficits, and the counting of gate receipts; and to be able to linger in my garden where the bright red and yellow apples weighted the trees earthward, lending a fragrance to the frosty air which is coupled with the crackling of wood-fires—nippy cold mornings—football games and Thanksgiving turkeys, while the whole of Autumn's joys were made more keen by the rough winds and sharpened sounds that spoke of the coming of winter.

Beauty and Friendship and the Dream Fulfilled.
—John Masefield.

Through the generous support of the patrons
and sponsors of the Philharmonic, California has
been given the opportunity to hear leaders of
superior rank interpret the masterpieces of the
music that has been written throughout the ages.

The visits of guest conductors are desirable as
we are detached, by distance, from other large
centres of art, and great benefit is reaped by our
musical public and our orchestra from the chance
to associate with the powers in the symphonic
world. A more serious attitude is developed
among the personnel of the orchestra as they become conscious that each new director assumes
that he is leading a competent group of musicians.
The leaders in turn are aware of the value of an
appearance before a new audience supported by a
good orchestra.

The importance of such an occasion is well
understood by Gabrilowitsch, who always refers
to the taste of his public when programs are made:

"Remember," he warns, "that the leader and the orchestra are only one half of the performance; the other half is made up of the audience."

Success in the West has furthered the career of several well-known artists. These men secured coveted places in localities which had been indifferent to their ability before California honored their genius. The respect and admiration that has been offered to leaders must stir them with a determination to return to their new territory again and to come back to it, if possible, more perfectly equipped than ever to merit its affection and its praise.

Our directors sway our imaginations with an interest only second to that which we feel towards the great composers. We follow their star long after it has moved to another horizon and with devotion we wait for its return to our midst.